MW01614247

The Halcyon Cry

Of
Cowboy Poetry
and Bagpipes

"Some people hear their own inner voices
with great clearness.
And they live, by what they
hear. Such people become 'crazy.'
They become legends ..."

Sioux Elder, 'One Stab'
Legends of the Fall

The Halcyon Cry

Of
Cowboy Poetry
and Bagpipes

Dr. Dennis L. Hunter

Credits:
Cover Design: Nicholas Corbin Swanson, Colorado Springs, Colorado
Text Design and Composition: Nicholas Corbin Swanson
Editor and Project Manager: Sharon Green, Panache Editorial,
                              Colorado Springs, Colorado
Cover Photo: iStock.com / Benjamin Schaeffer
Printed by: KC Book Manufacturing, Kansas City, Missouri

Copyright © 2019 by Dr. Dennis L. Hunter

All rights reserved. Printed in the United States of America. No part of this book may be used or reproduced by any mechanical, photographic, or electronic process, or in the form of a phonograph recording, nor may it be stored in a retrieval system, transmitted, or otherwise copied without written permission from the author except in the case of brief quotations embodied in critical articles and reviews. For information contact the author through Sacred Mountain Publishers.

This is the "public edition."

Available in both soft bound book and ebook formats.

ISBN: 978-09986902-2-3

Published by
Sacred Mountain Publishers
P.O. Box 3042
Grand Junction, Colorado 81502

http://www.cowboypoetryandbagpipes.com

Contents

Dedicated to

Kayla, Jason, Michael, Gwen and Caden

So that they might know their Grandfather.

Prologue

I Am Adesh; and I Am here.

I Am a Jnana Yogi; and a Priest of Jaguar Clan. I Am a Warrior of Wodan; and a Son of Thor. I embrace the Maha Mudra, and forge the path of Maha Dharma. I Am One, who would serve the Adnam.

For over 900 thousand years have I been on this Pilgrim's Quest. Countless empires have I seen—rising and falling. I have been many things in many places.

I have been thrust into the heights of honor, glory, and power. And I have been cast into the catacombs of perversion, degradation, and despair.

Come, sit with me now; for now is the time of the Revealing; for now is the time of the Healing.

Let us form a Great Circle. Let us celebrate the Many Paths. Let us learn to Worship the One God with One Voice.

Let us learn to serve one another, and thus fulfill the intention of Our Creator.

Introduction

So what's this all about ... ?

Many times when readers encounter one of my books, I hear them ask "So what's this all about." Of course, one way to find out is to simply read the book. That is why they are written.

It is a very human reaction to seek an immediate, simple quip in which the mind can quickly categorize and dispatch one of my books into something familiar, manageable, and perhaps more easily dispensable. In an age and culture replete with the incessant clamoring for our precious time and attention, it is not an unreasonable query. Time and attention is perhaps our dearest earthly commodity and should be spent wisely.

Decades ago, I was commissioned to write a trilogy of books by a woman, my wife, during one of her altered states of consciousness; speaking the words of a presence which simply referred to itself as the Source.

I entitled the first book *Telluride: The Sacred Valley*; the second, *The Priestess of Mokhi Maya*. Now I have written this third one: *The Halcyon Cry of Cowboy Poetry and Bagpipes*.

There are also a few published booklets of transcripts from her channeled readings. But that is mostly another subject, more suited for another time.

There is no cult. There is no organization. There is nothing to join and nothing to buy, except maybe a book. And, you can do with it as you wish. I lose money on every book that is sold. You can "Google" them, and yes they have been digitized.

In addition to sales, I have given away over three thousand books, usually one or two at a time, as the spirit moves me. They may be gifted to strangers I meet along the way, or perhaps left on a table, beside a trail or on a park bench, as I wander about in my travels.

Responses to my offerings are often of a gracious, but superficial thanks. Some are annoyed and perplexed, not understanding why I would do such a thing; perhaps not wanting to be bothered, and thinking they are being solicited or recruited for something. Some launch criticisms and outrage while scarcely glancing at the covers.

A treasured few declare themselves fans and followers and send me messages and letters of appreciation and gratitude. These are the ones for whom I write.

At times, I anonymously smuggle my books into stores and place them on shelves. And they sell them—while formally declining to order them, due to their exclusive corporate policies and restrictions on inventories. Subsequently, I occasionally discover my books on obscure websites though I have no direct knowledge of how they got there.

In this twenty-first century, book selling has become an extremely expensive and competitive venture. There are more and more books, and fewer and fewer readers. Most reading has transitioned to electronic devices, where summaries and headlines are predominately attended to and preferred. Specialized blogging and newsletters have become prevalent. Some studies suggest that less than 50 percent of purchased books actually get read.

Financially successful publications are usually created as an adjunct to a person of existing notoriety; or to add supposed legitimacy and bolster market share to an already established enterprise or service.

Of course well-marketed "how to" books of good quality on popular subjects such as dieting and cooking often do well. There are perhaps more "self-help" books available than there are people to read them. Large book sellers in concert with major publishers often have a stable of writers who can and do target demographics that cater to the most popular fads and lucrative subject matter—mining the niches that support the struggle to keep their doors open.

But, many a well-intended editor and/or publisher has gutted and destroyed the essential message of a spiritual masterpiece because of their ignorance or because it didn't support their personal worldview.

Had my three books been sown for commercial profit, they would have been written very differently. They would have been honed to meet the proverbial sixth-grade reading and educational level, both in sentence structure and vocabulary.

According to conventional wisdom, this is the capacity of comprehension of the general population; it makes for "good reads." I dispute that view. But if it be true, I propose that vocabulary and comprehension can be improved if presented in what I hope is an inspiring and thought-provoking manner.

My writing style is purposely designed to make you slow down; to ponder, evaluate and digest what you are reading. For some this could prove to be the most exasperating book that has ever been read. If that becomes you, try reading it out loud. Sometimes that allows a more natural flow, as if it were a conversation.

If commercial profit and notoriety were my principle aim, there would be seductive claims of secret knowledge that could be mastered in a few simple, easy-to-understand lessons.

There would be assertions that the reader would be propelled into esoteric states of cosmic consciousness; to be filled with wisdom, to be saved from damnation, while being guided by spirit that is holy; to receive uncommon insights and magical powers; to be imbued with abilities to have and to become whatever is desired.

Now all that is not necessarily a bad thing, and I'd like to think that I have been blessed with at least a smattering of some of that knowledge and ability.

These focused merchandizing approaches do spark interest and facilitate sales. Why not use them? Such claims certainly can and do catch my own personal attention and curiosity.

But this is just not what this series of three books is about. However, it is possible that reading them may yet add to those esoteric qualities which are so seldom mastered, yet so ardently sought.

This trilogy has been written to describe and to document a personal autobiographical journey from which readers can gather validating insights and expanding perspectives. These efforts will hopefully encourage or enhance the experiences of others who are embarked upon their own special journeys.

These books are not for everyone. Perhaps you will find nothing here of value. But, for a precious few there will be profound meaning for their lives. These books are for outlanders. Perhaps you are one of those.

Though most would scarcely believe it is possible, everything in the first two previous works (*Telluride – The Sacred Valley* and *The Priestess of Mokhi Maya*) has been about real people, places, and events. Considerable diligence and time was expended, going over every syllable, in relentless effort to ensure that these factual accounts were as accurate as I could make them.

Some aspects may seem too incredible to be considered, accepted, or believed. That too is alright. That does not mean that you are not on your own sacred journey; creating your own unique destination with your own magical discoveries. Not all trees grow alike or at the same rate, or in the same time or place.

Some folks have considered me to be a bit delusional, a con artist or even an outright liar; making it all up, seeking to defraud, or even intentionally consorting with demonic forces.

Others have attempted to declare me their teacher and occasionally have discovered the strangest things that I had never knowingly suggested or expected in my writings. To me, a well-written and intentioned book is as much a reflection of the reader as the author.

It is my most profound and sincere wish that you will enjoy and grow from whatever insight and meaning you may encounter as you travel through my pages.

When first I began to write, the Source exhorted me to eventually consider posing my works as fiction; for then, it is often easier for the population to consider, to accept certain possibilities into the culture. In this manner the consciousness of humankind has an opportunity to become expanded, enhanced, and enlivened.

It was explained to me that quite a number of authors and storytellers pose their tales as fiction, when in fact they are recounting actual experiences, sometimes from other times and places.

It can be almost impossible to get quality clearinghouses to publish a book if there is a claim that it is a true story. Their tendency is to believe the book is too peculiar and subsequently not a lucrative project. Thus, the birthing of the genre of "based on a true story." This phrase perhaps presents a more popular and acceptable approach, but often has little resemblance to the actual story.

It has been suggested that posing a true story as fiction reduces the natural resistance, the incredulity of an unbelieving mind, yet offers an opportunity to enjoy seeing things in a unique or expanded way. An odd or unusual tale can sometimes be more palatable and even inspiring if one isn't struggling with the dilemma of whether or not it is true.

That is also why some have preferred to teach in parables; to reveal concepts within cultures where conscious minds are not yet ready to consider, understand, or embrace expanded ways of knowing and being. It is why some teachings remain secret, so as not to be profaned by well-meaning, but errant antagonists, who are not yet ready to embrace the next step of the evolution of the soul in the earth.

After much reflection and meditation, I have decided to move on from the self-imposed constraints of the previous two books. I shall bow to the words, wisdom, and will of the Source. I shall accept and complete my contract; I shall fulfill my commission in accordance with that guidance that was offered so many decades ago.

So now, you may consider this present book a *mostly true, autobiographical novel*. I will allow the readers to grapple with its accuracy and authenticity. They do that anyway. Those who know me well will know the truth when they hear it. But you get to decide for yourself; and I don't have to assert, argue, or defend.

There is much of this journey that I will never be able to adequately express or explain. There is much that would not interest my fellow travelers, nor would they be ready to understand; but there are footsteps left in the sand for those who would follow.

This book was written in order to elucidate, validate, and inspire those who are on similar paths of their own. For, in truth, mere words do not teach; one must encounter, explore, and have one's own experiences in order to truly comprehend, master, and know. But that doesn't mean we can't offer occasional insights and guidance to one another.

The discerning, intuitive reader is invited to discover and enjoy a number of gems, hidden in plain sight, within this final edition. The relentlessly dedicated may find themselves called or summoned to search and seek meaning in their own interpretations of hidden codes and proofs concealed within the unfolding tapestry of this trilogy. Perhaps you will detect your own key to priceless treasure.

Chapter One

Jebudiah Ben McCreary

It was evening again, the time of twilight, myst and shadow; when the world becomes quiet and still, when moments linger between light and darkness. Where Spirit emerges intimate and complete, hanging suspended between coexisting realms, allowing glimpses into the fullness of a divine heritage. It is a time of blissful celebration; of a joyous soul, replete with heart-felt appreciation for a world of beauty, abundance, and joy.

His eyes were closed. He was drifting again between the eternities, where memories of both past and future events were stirring and coalescing back into his present. Vibrant and alive were the sights, sounds, and fragrances so remote, yet so familiar. The remembering created dancing eddies of flowing images and sensations, birthing thoughtful emotions debating, clamoring, sometimes frenzied, in desperate attempts to decipher the many visions, to make sense out of the "dreaming while awake."

He releases a long, ragged breath; rubbing his weathered face with his rough, gnarled hands and pulling his mesmerized mind back into his body. He climbs slowly out of his creaking rocker, stretches for a moment and stands upright and tall upon the split and sagging boards of his tiny veranda. He stares motionless, faithfully, toward the fading purple and orange of a distant horizon—as if watching for something, or perhaps some*one*.

Then, it wells up within him. He is engulfed by the forever vigilant and comforting presence. With soulful humility and a tear of heart-felt gratitude, he responds.

"Thank you, Precious Spirit. Thank you."

"I am here," he murmurs. "I am here."

This is Jeb, at his cloistered wilderness retreat. It was verbally deeded to him by a dying cavalry comrade, who had turned prospector after scouting for Reynolds and Crook during the Yellowstone and Big Horn Indian Campaign. It's a good place for hermitage; a place of healing, reflecting, and communing with spirits that are mostly sacred.

Here Jeb spent much time contemplating teachings and practices of the Florida Seminoles who had befriended him in his youth. During his expeditions and forays across the American West, he had also encountered other exotic peoples with cultures both magnificent and ancient.

The homestead was founded as a small tent-cabin with a tattered canvas roof, a few rough-sawn planks for walls, and an uneven flagstone floor. Originally, this served as a secluded, remote campsite where supplies could be protected from weather and predators; where they could be safely secured in the adjacent, hollowed-out canyon wall.

Taking refuge under the large existing cleft, beneath an overhanging cliff-face, it became a prospector's tunnel; laboriously carved to a length of some fifteen to twenty feet. The roof was low but opened into a small, oval-shaped, cave-like room approximately eight to ten feet across. It became a place where prayers and rituals were sometimes conducted.

At the portal was an artfully-crafted wooden door of heavy oak. It brandished a rusting chain with an intimidating, antique lock. However, the most effective security feature was the natural camouflage of plentiful, thick brush in partnership with the sun's interplay of shadow reflecting the uneven, twisted, and fractured features of the canyon's massive walls.

From this primitive outpost, seasonal expeditions embarked into the rugged alpine basins in quest of adventure, riches, gold, and sometimes something more; something much more, something of unending, eternal value.

Jeb's cabin is nestled just inside the curiously seductive entrance to this secluded, dog-legged canyon. It was built with respectful appreciation for the land, its seasons and vistas. The ground offers a formidable protective posture, making it an easy place to defend against ill-intended marauders. The structure straddles a naturally occurring, long, flat berm; cradled by an outcropping of red- and orange-stained rock that encases white, milky stringers of quartz, suggesting a promise of rich ore.

Although the walls are high and majestic, the whole canyon does not exceed but a hand-full of acres. During the chill of frozen winter mornings, the knoll receives the gift of warmth from the rising sun. During lazy summer afternoons there is relief from waves of stifling heat beneath a canopy of cool, refreshing shade; all this is enhanced by the playful rattling of a reliable mountain stream, meandering its way through the open ravine.

Spring thaws, or a generous monsoon, sometimes provoke a hidden waterfall into releasing delicate arrays of rainbows within its feathering myst. With this blessing, the anointed little valley grows green and fertile with an abundance of grasses, willow, aspen, and cottonwood. There is, of course, a multitude of nature's creatures coming to feed, drink, and raise their young; claiming their own sovereign homesteads.

In ancient times "the people" made pilgrimage to this place and brought with them their nourishing plants and healing herbs to complete nature's garden. Jeb seems mostly unaware of these visits and celebrations. But there are moments, dreaming moments, when he recalls their sojourns and joins with them—staring thoughtfully into the remnants of fading messages and memorials, etched into the timeless canyon walls—as he is coaxed, and once again begins to drift.

One night, during the fullness of a rising moon, he found himself chanting words and songs in a language that he did not know. They welled up from deep within him, like an unexpected flowering, struggling upward, claiming a birthright of eternal wisdom and joy.

The tones and rhythms surrounded him with a profound knowing that something or someone very sacred was present. He emerged feeling comforted and complete. As the years wore on, he often found himself doing things he didn't quite understand, but it never troubled him as long as he felt the comforting spirit beside and within him. He considered the spirit his most trusted friend and reliable companion.

The cabin was forged from stone and timber; assembled by strong, confident, gifted hands. Douglas fir posts and hand-hewn ponderosa rafters support a gentle sloping, flower-studded, sod-laden roof. Heavy log timbers set upon indestructible native rock form strong, protective walls, meticulously sealed with a home-made mortar of sunbaked clay and hand-chopped grasses.

At approximately four-hundred square feet, the structure features a long narrow bedroom along the back wall with its own private escape hatch into a small dugout cellar hidden beneath two-inch, hand-planed floor boards.

Generously-sized, rectangular windows, adorned by stout, reinforced shutters, offer an expansive view of the distant valley below; as well as glimpses into the majestic and unconquered alpine peaks above.

Out back, there's a serviceable outhouse, just past some tall willow bushes. It's a bit too close and there has been consideration to move it. But during a hard winter's night that might make it a bit too far away.

Jeb generally sleeps in the bunk across from the abandoned river-rock fireplace which has been reworked to accommodate a modest cast-iron cook stove. It was a welcomed improvement, for heating as well as cooking. It had been disassembled and packed-in with other supplies and staples the previous spring, via mule. That approach was easier than attempting to navigate a heavy wagon up into the ravine through a washed-out coulee and up along a narrow, rocky ledge.

Wrought from his own "ad lib" recipe, Jeb became a master at creating an evolving version of venison or salt-pork stew.

Included might be some partially sprouted potatoes from a frayed burlap bag, or a few recently harvested wild onions. Of course a variety of beans, a bit of flour and maybe a little rice was usually on the menu. Makings for soda biscuits or corn bread with a little molasses was always a great treat. He pretty much saw whiskey and tobacco as ceremonial or trade items, but coffee was a necessity. When coffee was gone he would collect and brew herbs and grasses in an effort to discover an acceptable tea.

He sometimes attempted a simple farmer's garden, but mostly foraged for a few indigenous vegetables, herbs, and spices if they were found in season, or could be dried and stored for later. He was always a little leery of mushrooms, feeling like you just don't want to make a mistake; and he didn't much see the point of grabbing something that likely as not might poison you.

Venison, rabbits and grouse were always in season. But watching the blood slowly drain from their still warm, and sometimes twitching, little bodies would often leave him feeling a bit sorrowful. Like many before him he would utter a short, contrite prayer and offer thoughts of thanksgiving for the sacrifice of their lives.

But he did like to eat. Enjoying a good feast, he would remember the endless, treacherous days on horseback when there were only sips of gritty, muddy water with some salted jerky, or moldy pemmican. Sometimes, there was no food at all.

He reflects on why a humane slaughter for food, and maybe a little leather, should make him feel uncomfortable; and, at times, more than just a little squeamish.

"After all, a man's gotta' eat, and sometimes you need a little fresh meat." And, we all know, "Somethin' has to die before somethin' else can live."

As a seasoned and capable cavalry scout, Jeb had witnessed and participated in considerable suffering and carnage during the skirmishes and battles he had encountered. He liked to believe, or more accurately, hoped, that at least some of his skillful scouting saved lives and perhaps averted even greater calamities.

He shudders and grimaces a bit, attempting to put behind him the scenes; the terrified eyes, the screams of agony; the twisted, mutilated visage of bodies frozen in time; often left bloated and rotting where they fell. These were reappearing, relentless images that would sometimes haunt him during the darkest times of his night.

He searches his memories and conscience and concludes once again, "Well, maybe that's the reason why huntin' has become such a bother to me."

There were also other images, other memories: decisive moments of boldness and tenacity; defining moments of challenge and sacrifice. These were glorious moments of honor and victory; covenants and loyalties forged within the crucible of battle. For better or for worse these are forever moments, stamped into eternity; deeds of triumph and glory, along with bittersweet moments of terror, heartbreak, and regret.

Jeb considered rounding up some fresh trout from the shallow pools between the intermittent riffles along the stream. He even built up the berm of a natural forming pond that nestled up against the arcing canyon wall, hoping it would induce a healthy crop of native trout. However, all he was able to snag were a few lost frogs and an occasional crawfish, which though nourishing was not all that appealing.

Over time, Jeb fashioned a crude fence from a collection of thick brush and parts of fallen trees. This kept his two horses and the mule trapped within the grassy coulee at bottom of the little box canyon. The simple, unrefined barrier also served as a place to gather fire wood when the "pickins" were slim.

He also upgraded a primitive shelter that once leaned against the west side of the ravine. It was an area where horses would catch the warmth of the morning sun and also be shaded from the heat in the afternoon. Jeb repurposed materials from the original, but now abandoned and collapsed cabin tent. Stacking loose sandstone, he completed a partial rock wall next to the existing outcropping. He reconstructed a roof utilizing old planking, lashing some of it together with random strips of frayed canvas.

Twisted and broken aspen rails along with other discarded materials were used to form an acceptable paddock, now complete with a shed for tack. The structure served its purposes, but the rotting roof and tattered canvass didn't do much to keep out melting snow or the drizzle of an occasional monsoon.

⊛   ⊛   ⊛

During the last few days, flocks of geese are seen looming overhead, wending their way south from the great Canadian shield. Remnants of yellow, gold, and orange aspen leaves flutter and shimmer in the bright sun while cascading to the ground, creating a carpet of bronze and gold. The foothills are alive with echoes of bugling elk and battling, grunting bucks gathering their harems for the annual rut.

The lush green of the high mountain slopes has faded; turning brown, auburn, and crimson. Dark billowing clouds cling to distant peaks, releasing a fog of feathery white flurries. The blessing of fresh snow creeps down the rocky ridges and into the silent alpine basins. Sacred mountains ready themselves for another, sleepy, frozen embrace.

There is a numbing chill to the air. Morning ice lingers at the edges of the little stream that flows just below the cabin. He wonders how he will get through the winter. He is thinking to himself: "This is no place for a solitary old cavalry scout, no matter how great he may have been in his day." As he fondles a few remaining gold coins in his pouch, he is thinking, "It's time to head back down, maybe to a town somewhere."

He needs to earn some wages for a renewed stake for the next spring; maybe a scouting job, just one more time. He could look to hire on at a ranch, if he couldn't find anything else. The 2nd and 3rd Cavalry has been ruthlessly hunting down the "renegades" after the Custer massacre. But there are so many brutal memories around Fort Fetterman. He no longer has the heart for it. And, the windswept prairies of Wyoming are no place for an old man to be in the winter. He's done that before.

Maybe he could sign on to get some more government survey work, if they haven't finished up yet. The army might need someone with both scouting and survey experience. But those are not expeditions for the winter months. That would most likely resume in the spring.

Every year the world seems to be moving faster; more people, more scars upon the land. Times are passing him by. He wonders if maybe he should winter someplace like Taos, Durango, Cheyenne, or even Denver. He wonders what he would do there. He thinks maybe there is no longer any place for him. He wonders where he would be if he had made different decisions.

His thoughts turn to his childhood home. His father, a Scots-Irish tacksman, worked a small plantation outside of Asheville in North Carolina. He was a grim, unhappy man who never seemed to have time for anything or anybody but his work.

The generation before, Jeb's grandfather, had been exiled to America to become a seven-year, involuntarily indentured servant, courtesy of the British Empire. Considering his struggle, Jeb's father had come a long way and was fortunate.

However, his father did not survive the war. His home and buildings—barns, stables and modest slave quarters—had been burned to the ground. When Jeb returned to Asheville he discovered that the remainder of the family farm had been seized by northern carpetbaggers for taxes.

With great fondness, he recalls growing up "next door" to "Lissy," named after the amaryllis flower. She came from an old southern family of considerable wealth and influence. Jeb became a sort of big brother to Lissy. She adored her father and would constantly praise his wisdom and virtues. She was living on a large remote plantation that was short on socially suitable playmates.

Lissy's father was a wealthy financier and an active abolitionist. Jeb had become a bit of a protégé, taken under his wing as the son he had always wanted. He contributed to and encouraged the lad's education, formal as well as informal. Jeb was allowed to accompany him on extended trips to large cities up north; watching first hand, how the business of preparing for war, a civil war, was being conducted.

Lissy's father was intimately involved in the politics of international trade between the Americas and Europe. He was a part of the growing rift between North and South; often called upon to make introductions and provide contacts; sometimes unofficially passing along politically sensitive messages.

As the war approached, Lissy was eventually sent to a prestigious finishing school for young ladies in France. Her father had purchased a small residence in Paris where he had been regularly visiting and conducting business.

After bitter quarrels with his younger brothers, her father re-established the family compound with most of their holdings somewhere up north. There were attempts at freeing many of the family's African slaves. Unfortunately, the political and legal climate of the South at that time meant that they had no place to go.

So, although freed, most remained on the plantation doing what they had always done, but as hired workers instead of slaves or indentured servants. In that process, Jeb also became familiar with the quiet, unseen, underground communities providing safe passage and sanctuary for Native American and African refugees. This is also where he was introduced to teachings that were Shamanist in nature; teachings that captured his imagination, heart, and soul.

After secession Jeb never saw Lissy or her family again. He was grateful for both the formal and informal education he received, and for the many trips he was able to take with her family. With the influence of Lissy's mother, Jeb had once considered becoming a protestant minister.

However, when secession was declared, as a loyal son of the South, Jeb was offered an officer's commission in the Confederate infantry. But Jeb, as a man of conscience and conviction, became a Union cavalry scout.

Superiors found him useful in providing information for assessing logistical strengths and weaknesses. He seemed gifted, or at least lucky, in selecting safe and expedient escape routes for the cavalry's penetrating reconnaissance raids in and out of his homeland. In the beginning, some were wary of his loyalties. He tended to stay to himself, which made his comrades even more suspicious. But after a few successful raids, his conflicts and loyalties were understood, and neither was questioned.

All that seemed like a lifetime ago. Jeb's destiny had drawn him ever westward to embrace all the adventure and promise that the expanding young nation had to offer.

Now, he is inspecting and repairing his tack; readying two horses and a mule for departure. After doing an inventory of remaining provisions he decides to leave a couple of extra blankets, some staples, and half dozen bulging tins still left over from his last campaign.

He leaves a well-stacked horde of firewood on the veranda and a freshly cut stash of dry kindling inside, next to the stove. It's just good manners to set things up for some lost and desperate pilgrim who might even be you.

He is feeling a tug, a drawing, a knowing. He will be exploring the Arizona territories for a while. He will wander down south, to and through half a dozen fledgling forts and outposts and maybe hold up at that garrison in the Verde Valley. He might find something to do there, and it's a lot warmer in the winter. Jeb is 44 years old. This is the closing of the year 1879.

Jeb doesn't know it yet, but there is talk about General Crook returning to the Arizona Territory where, before the Custer massacre, he built a reputation for dealing fairly with the Indians and keeping them on the reservations, preserving the peace, and setting up "Indian Agencies." He made good attempts at doing the right thing with the Apache tribes, even within the throes of political persuasions to the contrary.

Crook knows Jeb, and owes him for the time when Reynolds was abandoned and there were no Indian scouts to be found. Jeb and two other white, civilian cavalry scouts had been enlisted, entreated by Gibbon, Terry, and Crook, to search through the "Bad Lands," to find out what was happening. What was found was more trouble than the impetuous Custer would be able to handle.

Jeb does not know it yet, but destiny has more chapters for him. He is headed to Tombstone, Bisbee, Fort Grant, San Carlos, and the Chiricahua Mountains. Once again, he will be scouting, riding for General Crook.

As he slow trots down the trail, in the splendor of his western paradise, Jeb starts to get that funny feeling again; he stretches and shrugs his shoulders, again. You see, he's sometimes conscious of me, "watching" him.

I feel the weight of my body nestled into the cozy mattress within my little travel trailer. I find myself stirring back into twenty-first-century awareness.

In the distance, I am hearing the halcyon cry of an antiquated narrow gage locomotive as it heralds its arrival into the center of modern day Silverton, Colorado. The train carries a precious cargo: a new wave of fun-loving adventure-seekers and explorers, some with a little money in their pockets, to sustain the local recreational economy.

I am back, cradled within the power of the San Juan Mountains, near the sacred valley. This day the presence of Jeb has been strong. I have recalled another day in the life of Jeb; one of the many facets of this soul.

I have been drifting, "remembering" again. I get up and gaze through the window. Yes, I am back. I stare with joyous appreciation at the splendor of granite peaks, and the luminous blooming of autumn colors. I marvel at the paradise that I am allowed to enjoy.

My little coyote brother, my four-footed companion, is in need of some adventure time of his own; perhaps down by the river, where the world is alive, fresh and flowing.

I pause for a moment, pondering Jeb's journey, then continue with my own.

Chapter Two

Soul Whispers

For twenty-nine years I was married to an extraordinary lady who, to our surprise and occasional apprehension, became a fully conscious psychic channel. That statement will mean different things to different people, depending on their own personal experiences and assumptions about such things. The source of this phenomena simply referred to itself as the Source, explaining that it had been known by many different names throughout different times and cultures.

My wife and I had many marvelous adventures and awakenings together. There were historical accountings, guided teachings with pilgrimages to sacred places, where we had the opportunity to have our belief systems challenged and reaffirmed; we were offered opportunities to learn and grow in understanding and purpose. We were immersed, protected and escorted into a whole array of alternative realities that challenged and expanded our perspectives in ways that are still unfolding.

In another time or place the Source of this experience might have been referred to as the Holy Spirit. Throughout the millennia, it has too often been maligned and misunderstood, whether it be by the redeemed in Christ, witnessing to an inner voice, supposedly speaking in tongues, or the testimony of its presence through the teachings and utterances of a child of nature. A faithful god speaks to all generations.

In a different milieu such a connection could be cause for suspicion of a pejorative something called witchcraft, which can make one worthy of being plunged into and held under water, time and time again until "confession" or death. Of course, there was always the time-honored tradition of being publically lashed to a pole, writhing and screaming in torment, within flames fanned by self-righteous assumptions of the easily frightened and pompously ignorant.

Crucifixion can come in many forms. Fortunately, most are eventually forgiven; "... for they know not what they do." Indeed, may He forgive us all.

But all that is another story; a story told within the book, *The Priestess of Mokhi Maya*. And this current story is a different story; or, perhaps an evolution of the same story.

While traveling in the late nineteen-eighties, I stopped to explore an old museum on the front range of the Colorado Rockies. As I sought a quiet moment on a weathered bench, I became acutely aware of another presence. Somehow, I could see into his mind; see what he saw, feel what he felt; understand what he knew and thought.

The connection lasted for the next several days, sometimes being stronger than at other times. Whenever, I closed my eyes or became a bit unfocused he would be there. I would be with him, alongside and within him all at the same time.

At first, there was a bit of trepidation regarding the significance and ramifications of such an experience. I could sense that though he was aware of me, it was to a lesser degree. I began to look into his life, and occasionally he was allowed into mine and we would marvel. The process seemed to provide us time to digest and adapt to the experience as we went along our mundane daily tasks.

I trusted that through the influence of the Source, I would gain greater understanding of the phenomenon over time. Later, I realized that Jeb was very intuitive himself and had his own First-People teachers and initiations. His strong foundation in progressive Protestantism had led him to consider Christian ministry. For a while, he had once been engaged in formal pastoral studies.

Sporadically, I would continue to "see" him, what he was doing and feeling; his thoughts and concerns, all wrapped inside a holy comforting presence. We were somehow allowed to connect, digest, and adjust to the process. There seemed to be a third force orchestrating, mentoring the unfolding embrace. It was not something I could make happen. It was something that I am sometimes enabled to allow to happen.

There are also times, places, and experiences that are blocked by this comforting, affirming benevolent presence; blocking that which would be of little value or possibly cause turmoil and confusion to decisions that would be made and that didn't need to be revisited again, from another time with different information.

Thus, was my introduction to Jebudiah Ben McCreary.

The Source of my wife's channeling explained that this was a naturally evolving process for the entity (me) and that it was intended, in part, to help me understand and experience what the channel (my wife) had encountered.

I was told it would serve to widen and strengthen the opening of my own questing soul. The words were something like that. These were words spoken many years ago, but I recall the concepts quite well.

It was explained that the purpose of such was not to just have an experience; but to have a personal witnessing to the profound connectedness and interactivity of the seen and unseen worlds within a multiverse of unlimited potential.

It was described as a by-product of the heralding, of the birthing process of a new age which is more accurately termed the "evolving next age." It was explained that a great harvest was coming into the earth of souls clamoring for liberation and redemption in which the Messianic spirit would be released.

Later, after my beloved's transition, she would sometimes come to me, offering comfort saying over and over, "See how it works; See how it works." She was sharing with me what it is like to experience communication from behind the veil as an expression of an ever-widening universe that the world is about to experience in more and more profound ways. Such are the harbingers of that divine presence whose earthly influence will continue to expand.

As a young child I remember lying in a huge bed in the quiet darkness. I could feel another body dwelling within and around my earthly, fleshly body. I could feel stretching or breathing sensations in this extra body that was dwelling within and around the earthly, flesh body. Occasionally, it would vibrate, twist, or spin.

At times, it felt like I was wiggling my toes inside my shoes or my fingers inside warm gloves. But this was like wiggling my whole body within an alternative parallel body. I could shrink, be very tiny, the size of small ball, or expand to the size of the whole room. It wasn't so much making it happen, as it was watching it happen; participating by allowing it to emerge and not feeling fearful or wishing to stop it.

Sometimes there would be warm sensations; sometimes cool ones. Sometimes I would feel tight; sometimes loose and floppy. There might be pulsing, sparkling sensations with an awareness of tiny lights twinkling like stars in a universe all around me and even inside of me—a whole variety of colorful manifestations, intimately swirling together. It would sometimes form a soft glowing myst that I could feel and move through.

Through these transitory veils and mysts there were sometimes visitations. Occasionally, I would become subtly, or even acutely, aware of an unseen spirit or entity who might launch, or simply watch with me, a variety of sensations and impressions that would permeate and linger. Sometimes they would leave me drifting blissfully within a timeless nurturing presence.

Throughout the lifetime, I have often sensed a presence that seems to stand watch over me as a sort of guardian; certainly during times of turmoil and emotional trauma, but especially during joyous times. Such visitations seemed to be celebrations to mark a particular accomplishment, or to validate the ending of one phase of my life and the beginning of another. For much of my adult life, I would ignore or push these experiences to the background of my memory, considering it just fanciful imagination.

Susan's Source would admonish me to trust these sensations, intuitions, and visitations claiming that most of the time my impressions were accurate. It was explained that as the lifetime progressed these experiences would become clearer and stronger.

She predicted that there would be more sensitivity to the ethereal energies, where thought forms dwell, as well as the spirit realms. This would be true for me and many, many others, within this and the coming generations.

When I was around four years of age I remember my grandmother telling my mother that I had an imaginary playmate. I didn't know what an imaginary playmate was. Then, I realized she must be talking about Elmer, a patient and kindly old gentleman who wore the overalls of a farmer. He liked to watch us play. Sometimes I would feel him smiling as he placed his hand on my shoulder.

At some point, it was determined that it was time for Elmer to leave. My mother became more than a little annoyed when she came looking for me and discovered that I and two friends were enthusiastically digging up her treasured flower bed. Although concerned, she also seemed a bit amused when I explained that we were burying Elmer.

We were in the process of conducting a funeral. I don't think I knew what a funeral was but, from the best I can remember, I knew it had something to do with people who died.

Soon after Susan's transition I traveled to Iowa to visit relatives I had not seen since I was a child; these included a few remaining cousins, an aunt, and my favorite uncle. Being interested in genealogy, I was also seeking out the final resting place of some of my more recent ancestors.

I found a beautiful old cemetery that had been founded during the mid-1800s, during the pioneer era. It was a well-cared-for piece of land with dark-green grass, set on a series of gently cascading hills. It was graced with a variety of tall, massive trees, many with thick, stout trunks. They left me thinking about oak groves and Druids.

I recall peaceful breezes, surging through fluttering leaves of gently swaying branches, stirring the oppressively humid air of a lazy summer day. I was learning to play bagpipes. To complete the pilgrimage I decided to conduct a memorial serenade at the graveside of my father's Scottish ancestors.

Leaving the gravesite of my great, great grandparents, I happened down a walkway and began feeling a tingling on my arms and across my back and shoulders. The hair on the back of my head felt like it was filled with an electrostatic charge; it felt like it was standing up.

I walked toward the gravestone that was drawing me like a magnet. My eyes were transfixed upon a finely-crafted, but modest monument that had captured my unwavering attention. As I stumbled around to the other side, I discovered a familiar name, crisply and deeply etched into the polished granite. It was Elmer.

After a moment of recollection and prayer, I involuntarily struck up my pipes and wistfully played "Amazing Grace," to honor my friend and childhood "playmate." In a sense I was burying him again.

Almost immediately I felt his familiar hand on my shoulder and remembered his smiling gaze.

Later, I discovered that this had been a distant relative; a cousin of a grandmother, if I remember correctly, on the farming side of the family. He had passed away a few years before I was born.

As I retreated down the worn walkway, I half felt and half heard the familiar voice of Susan, whispering in my spirit.

"See how it works; See how it works."

Chapter Three

Malcolm's Castle

He is disoriented and bewildered. He is not sure where he is, or where he has been. He has awakened and is resisting any temptation to stray back into slumber. He thinks he might have been dreaming.

Nothing makes sense. There is no recognition or understanding of the place where he has found himself. In the mydst of this clouded stupor he attempts to survey his unfamiliar surroundings. Briefly, he considers that the haunting dream may not yet have ended. He has been within this state of mindless wandering for some time; perhaps for years. The perception of time has been flexing and eroding. He does not yet acknowledge that he has been loosed to another dimension, another realm of existence.

The black-maned mare had faithfully returned the barely conscious Scot, back to more sympathetic grounds. Bloodied and weak, the young warrior collapsed to the ground. He instinctively lapped up a fresh trickle of water before crawling clumsily through the brush and mud, and into the shelter. It was a crudely constructed storage room nestled into a tree-lined outcropping next to River Tay.

When the tide was full, a shallow, handdug canal of some fifty meters provided direct access to the river. The primitive structure was hewn from a rock face, half-cave and half-masonry, with a low hanging ceiling. The shelter was suited to store produce and home-crafted goods. A smoky black patina clung to the overhanging rock, bearing witness to open fires, suggesting occasional habitation or signaling.

Across the threshold was a poor-fitting, wooden door that opened to a squatty pier. Rotting timbers were encased in dank soil; they were unevenly covered with a collection of flat rocks, forming a barely adequate loading dock. Small wooden boats could gather and deliver goods and supplies, and perhaps small livestock, in the pursuit of an agrarian cottage industry of late-seventeenth-century Scotland.

Once again, times were turbulent. Perhaps they always were. An uprising was afoot and many a Laird had been called upon to provide an offering of fighting men. The adventurous clansman, fiercely loyal to both family and Laird, had been recruited and led by a local tacksman, who had known and guided the young lad since birth.

Malcom the Tacksman, as he was known, was an almost perfect specimen of fine Scottish manhood. He stood close to six feet tall, was stout, and agile even in his maturing years. He had angular hawk-like features with a smooth, ruddy complexion; and shoulder-length, light-brown hair. It sported a slight reddish hue, especially when captured by sunlight. He was known as an honest and fair-minded man and greatly respected, with a reverence usually reserved for a clergyman. He was known for successfully managing disputes between local clan folk; and he served as an agricultural overseer for his own lands, as well as that of his Laird's.

However, there was a tendency to assume responsibility that was never his own. He considered himself to be a gifted matchmaker, which occasionally rendered some rather humorously, dubious results.

To his credit, he believed it was his duty to assure that every able-bodied soul within his domain had a vocation, enough to eat, and a safe place to sleep and call home. He had a particular calling to seek out youngsters in whom he saw potential for greatness. He would mentor them with substantial passion and enthusiasm. In short, he was what many would call a good man.

However, some saw these tendencies as meddling, over-reaching; even to the point of undermining the authority of his own ruling Laird and benefactor. But most saw these characteristics as welcomed concern and affection for those of the shire. For the greater part, his efforts at administration were so productive and successful that his superiors were willing to give him a free hand with only an occasional summons for routine oversight or respectful censure.

His Achilles' heel, obvious to all, was a fierce sense of pride and honor which he treasured above all else. He was outspoken and confident of the supremacy of his own beliefs. He was rather sensitive about his humble beginnings and the loss of his father in battle; allegedly due to his sire's indecision and cowardice.

If his motives were publically questioned, even casually; Malcolm could become enraged, offering no quarter to any adversary. Only with the passage of considerable time, along with contrite and repentant gestures, would he consider forgiving any offending party. It was said that Malcom had a long memory.

Fortunately, his wife, the Clan Chief's youngest sister, had a gift. She always knew how to approach and what to say to soothe her husband's sometimes inflamed and wounded soul. It was quietly believed that she was the balancing wisdom behind his mastery as a problem-solver, mediator, and mentor.

Spurred by the early calamities of the rise of the Stuarts to political prominence, Malcolm was commissioned to raise and lead a band of militant Highlanders to answer the call to arms. His task was to reinforce a floundering Scottish army, gathered to stand in the face of oppression. And, it provided a welcomed opportunity for Malcolm to demonstrate his unwavering dependability and loyalty. Through claiming his own glory, perhaps his father's lost honor could be salvaged while steadfastly affirming his own honor, along with the exorcising of a few personal demons.

Malcolm's charisma and reputation drew a force of some thirty-five zealots and half-hearted discontents. Some were volunteers and some were volunteered. There were only seven horses among them, along with two small, but ample, carts that carried scant food and other hastily confiscated provisions.

Less than twelve were experienced veterans of the "run-hide" style of guerrilla warfare, for which Highlanders were famous. Most had weapons of a sort, gleaned from previous campaigns; perhaps hand-me-downs from previous generations. On the whole, musketry was a very personal and unorganized endeavor. Some weapons were fashioned from farming implements. Battle axes were popular.

There were a number of archers and several men who knew the effective art of the pike. The majority tended to be those who knew how settle disputes with the swing of a fist, the poke of a staff, or a bit of slashing with cutlery. Few had mastered the manly art of slaying an adversary with the broad blade of a claymore on the battlefield; or anywhere else, for that matter. Many had never been more than a day's walk from where they were born.

There had been little time for training, establishing organization, or discipline. Malcolm had previous tutelage and experience as an acting war chief. He quickly appointed a cadre of sorts to marshal and manage the growing mob that had responded to their Laird's summons. Also present was a gaggle of servants and domestics—would-be camp followers. But their participation was not encouraged.

Among the neophytes was a lad who Malcom had proudly mentored. The young scholar had just returned from a season with the monks at the abbey in Iona where Malcolm was sponsoring his education. He was like a son to him, as they say; especially since Malcolm had no sons of his own. He vowed to keep the eager apprentice close so he could instruct him, and perhaps keep him safe as well. But mostly; he wanted the lad close because Malcolm knew he could be trusted.

So, on a blustery, sun-filled day, the rag-tag band struck out across the highlands to march to their fate; which was to be played out in Dunkeld, some hundred miles distant. At first the group moved swiftly, almost euphorically, in a frenzy to locate the main body. It was assumed that the contingent would rally with the main army; there they would receive their orders and assignment for engagement.

It became clear; at least to Malcolm, that his instructions had been vague and incomplete. It was hard to know what forces were where, and when they might rendezvous. Scottish groups of all persuasions were on the move. Their precise intentions and locations were unknown to him. Along the way "conscripts" of dubious loyalties joined the band and seemed to only add to the growing speculations.

While meandering through the countryside, it wasn't easy to know who was friend and who was foe. News came by happenstance which could, at best, be relied upon as rumor. And anyone who could offer a bit of tactical or logistical information, could just as easily give away your own capacities and intentions toward your adversaries.

Due to the lack of clarity of the mission and growing fatigue, dissention and rebellion began to eat away at Malcolm's rag-tag command. Beginning on the fourth day the weather had turned Scottish. It was miserable. Along with the drizzle and damp came the cold and the accompanying boggy mud with swarms of biting and blood-sucking insects. Rationed food was dwindling. Feet were bruised and bleeding. Some talked of going home.

Nevertheless, his band had grown to over fifty men at arms; along with a woman; most felt she was a little deranged. She was savagely independent and followed ancient and pagan ways. She had joined them with her son and two militant daughters who were also bearing arms. Malcom reluctantly accepted them into the fold, surmising that no ill-intentioned man would dare touch them. He watched them with much amusement and curiosity. But that is yet another story woven into the tapestry of the time.

Though personally troubled, Malcom continued to offer his command an uplifting outlook; he enthusiastically expounded on how they would succeed and engender much favor if they would stick together and support one another. He would remind them that they were all duty-bound to Chief and Laird to complete the campaign. As always, Malcolm carefully watched and listened.

The band had stopped next to a modest ravine where fresh water and game were abundant. The site was likely selected because of the great trees and lush foliage which served to offer seclusion for the encampment. It was a good place to bivouac, rest, and regain strength; Malcom made his assessment for the next step.

However, Malcom's authority and leadership were being steadily undermined. Blame was actively being assessed and expressed. The men were mostly ready for capitulation; and the campaign had barely started. And again, as always, Malcom was watching and listening. His wrath was beginning to stir.

On the seventh day, as fate would have it, a uniformed courier who had lost his way came stumbling into camp. Malcolm immediately detained him and began to question him intensely, with a veracity that astonished some of his cadre.

It seemed that a skirmish had taken place less than three hours away. The opposing armies were assembling and angling for a major battle that was sure to come at any time.

Though it was rumored that there was dissension within the Jacobite leadership, it was also reported that the opposing alliance might be crumbling. The Cameronian Governmental Regiment commander had been slighted, relieved of command, and replaced by a young upstart.

This treacherous regiment of well-trained and supplied professional soldiers hailed from the southern lowlands. It had grown out of a protestant religious movement which some referred to as fanatical because it opposed the mostly Catholic Highlanders. It was a regiment encouraged by the Sassenach (Saxon-English) government.

The Cameronians had a reputation for quickly dispatching prisoners. Their campaigns were brutal, even genocidal. Some Highlanders had scores to settle. It was close to a religious war and the government in power was willing to use this feud to its own advantage.

It just so happened that this controversial movement's inspired leader was named Cameron, but he had nothing to do with Clan Cameron. He was a blight upon the name of Cameron, for this regiment had been formed using the Cameron name without clan permission or participation. This crusade stood in opposition to the values of traditional Scottish Highlanders. Many of Clan Cameron would eventually fight against this perceived perversion and become champions for the Jacobite cause.

Nevertheless, on this day it became Malcolm's understanding that there was a plausible dispute of whether or not this misguided, misnamed regiment would continue to stand strong against the Highlanders.

The previous day, in the ravine next to the camp, Malcolm had found a horse wandering loose and missing a rider. He commandeered the animal and gave it to his young friend and protégé, assigning him duties as a scout. He was given the mission to advance as far forward as personal safety would permit, and bring back critical information needed to determine where and if it was safe to rendezvous.

That same evening the young lad came galloping back to Malcom with great excitement. His heart was filled with ecstasy. What he had discovered with his own eyes was exactly what Malcom needed to know. He had encountered many motley bands of Highlanders, much like their own, emerging from the great forests, gathering and converging on the hills and ridges above Dunkeld. It seemed the entire Highland army was massed and uniting at this gateway to the highlands. They were all responding to the call of the flaming Highland cross. The clans were finally uniting.

So, based upon the information at hand; common sense dictated that now was a time for decision. Malcolm concluded he should continue south toward Perth. He reasserted his authority, rallied his grumbling militia, and flung them southward with great haste. His enthusiasm and decisiveness dispelled much of the dissension and brought the band to a sense of unity and renewed commitment.

It was anticipated that many hundreds of swarming Jacobites were about to surround the town. The encircled governmental regiment would be vulnerable to the great Highland charge. They would be cut off. Any reinforcements from Perth would be too little too late.

Half walking and half running, hearts pounding with excitement, Malcolm's little band comes alive. The slow and clumsy carts, along with the pack horses, handlers and followers, are left behind to catch up later.

Mounted, Malcolm leads his emerging mob from the front of the pack. With hope and glory, shining in his eyes, the young scout has been sent ahead with two other riders, experienced in selecting and clearing a path for those following on foot.

The afternoon breezes swell through the swaying trees, as rustling, rattling leaves herald the Highlanders' approach. The sun flickers and darts through the canopy as they scurry through the great, green forests above Dunkeld. Adrenaline is high. Their bodies become soaked in welcomed cooling sweat. There is a rhythmic beating of feet upon the soft loam of the damp forest floor. There are heavy murmurs and sighs mixed with the rise and fall of cyclic, heavy breathing as the troop pounds its way toward glory.

This is rapidly becoming Malcolm's great moment. In his mind's eye he sees himself leading a great Highland charge, wading victoriously into the enemy. His primal emotional conflicts are overcoming his temperance and prudence. His reason is shutting down and giving into his considerable passions. All he can know and feel is: this is his moment. Nothing will dissuade him.

Suddenly, bursting through the underbrush come two of his horsemen, franticly bouncing and weaving through the old-growth woodland. Briefly they stop, panicked and winded. They have blustered into the dreaded Sassenach cavalry, which is rallying, conducting a sortie to break the momentum of arriving clansmen. They had hoped to disrupt the Highlanders' ability to rendezvous and move into the relative safety of the growing encampment: the huge gathering that was spreading across the hills and the ridges above Dunkeld.

The Cavalry of Lord Cardoss is bounding forward and will soon collide with the disorganized, little band. It is not clear if Malcolm's scouts have been seen or are being pursued. But the forefront of Malcom's column has witnessed their terror. It becomes contagious. Malcolm leaps into action, exclaiming that all should immediately follow him.

"We can run-hide, if they cum' pun' us," he bellows, resolute and wild-eyed.

He expects that if the government cavalry should come their way, he can let them pass by quickly, using his horsemen to draw their attention away from his infantry in hiding.

He stands his ground, commanding those on foot to run toward the edge of a little berm, and down into the briary thickets of the overgrown ravine where horses may not be so willing to venture. He bids them to conceal themselves among the fallen trees and dense underbrush.

There, they can lay, still; quiet in the safety of the tall grass and gullies, and allow government cavalry to gallop past them unaware; the Highlanders covered and camouflaged by their muted tartan plaids.

His frenzied scouts ignore their commander and bolt creating chaos and triggering a flurry of frightened clansmen stampeding mindlessly through the forest in all directions. Malcolm immediately brands them all as cowards and deserters.

Those who have been charged with leadership are contributing to a collapse of discipline rather than responding to a call for a focused rally from their legitimate and adept commander. A few of the band stand with Malcom. The rest go noisily crashing through the forest, with no thought of anything except to flee along with the mutinous mounted cadre.

Then, Malcolm's trusted protégé comes galloping out of the wood and into the mydst of the maddening chaos. Riding immediately to his mentor's side, he instantaneously grasps the situation. Decisively, he spurs his steed in pursuit; he intends to turn the stampede and return the mob to good order. But as he turns away, Malcolm sees only that his young protégé is also deserting him. After all Malcom has done for him and has hoped for him, he is betrayed.

Malcolm goes mad with a vengeance and a fury of the damned. Rage erupts from the depth of his belly. His large, dark eyes almost flashing red, veins pulsing out of his neck, a death defying battle cry explodes form the depths of his very soul.

He resolutely refuses to be defeated.

He swings wildly, with the outstretched tip of his halberd staff, slashing at the young protégé, striking him in the shoulder, slicing across his back and down his side toward his abdomen, then toppling him from his mount.

Those nearby are startled and stunned at the speed and decisiveness of the tragic event. They stand and stare motionlessly in disbelief, not knowing how, or if, they should respond. The young warrior tumbles to the ground moaning and writhing, the first casualty of their campaign.

Then, the wise woman lunges forward with her progeny, urging them to lift the young ranger to his saddle. Clumsily, he is draped across the back of his panicked and prancing steed.

He collapses upon his saddle with arms flailing around his horse's neck. Hands instinctively clutch at the mane. Quickly, he is carried into the darkening woodland.

Malcolm sits as a statue, so stunned by the event that he does not move. It is as if he does not even comprehend what has transpired and who had committed such a dreadful atrocity. He is in shock, witnessing what his rage has wrought. He will linger there for longer than he cares to remember; on that day he became an entrapped, tortured, anguished soul.

With the arrival of government cavalry, Malcolm pivots his grey gelding and follows Colin into the forest; thus repenting, hoping to find forgiveness and redemption. Neither of them ever see their beloved highlands again.

The fragile little band of deserters was left totally vulnerable; to be run down by the red-coated dragoons of Lord Cardoss.

Eventually, most of Malcolm's volunteers were dispatched or rendered harmless. Survivors crawled and stumbled back, in disgrace, toward their distant Highland homes; they never reached the rattle of muskets within the embattled hamlet below.

Straight away and without clarity of forethought the cavalry was recalled to Perth by Colonel Ramsey. The Jacobites did overrun Dankeld; but not long after, the Cameronians took it back again. The government soldiers burned down the town completely, slaughtering over three hundred Scots in the process. The so-called Cameronians jeered, chanted and sang psalms, and recited scripture at the fleeing, "heathen" Highlanders. During the savagery of the siege, a contingent of Scots was locked in a building and burned alive.

Perhaps it is the anthem of Scotland, or of humanity itself, that first you win, then you lose. Then you win, and lose again; then you wait for another time to persevere once more.

The little shipping point was concealed at the bottom of a cliff-lined ravine of less than two acres. Massive trees flourished above the dark green of the overgrown tangle of vegetation. A narrow path wound its way around the cliffs and along the edge of the outcroppings toward the castle grounds.

Not really a castle, as we might think of it today. As are most historic compounds, it has undergone several additions and remodels through the centuries. It was perhaps small for a castle, but a bit large for a simple great house for a Laird and family that once supported the Jacobite cause. It is perhaps best described as a fortified mansion where a noble Scottish family survived for over three hundred years.

Though unpretentious, it was a castle indeed, complete with protective stone walls and parapets gracing the four-story pele tower. It was a habitation with many fine rooms—sporting a great hall, with a winding staircase, barrel ceilings, and fine furnishings. There was an enormous kitchen on the first floor complete with quarters for those who served the Laird's household.

Though a modest Lordship, it was obviously a robust household; productive and lively.

Just outside the protective castle walls were over thirty ancillary structures: thatch-and-stone living quarters, stables and pens for livestock, facilities for craftsmen, and of course abundant gardens with wee crofts sprawling across the rolling green hills.

This was a secluded, but not isolated, staging area where sometimes goods and services were received or shipped. Sometimes folks would simply gather to exchange the latest news. From here you could make your way, by river, into the city center in Perth, or perhaps travel down river toward Dundee.

I had come upon the grounds by accident; the result of taking a wrong turn on a roundabout along the A9. It was my second trip to Scotland. I had taken lodging next to the Hungry Horse Pub. They had marvelous, wholesome, hearty food and a pleasant, inviting atmosphere which I very much enjoyed. Being a little travel weary, I booked the room for three nights and hoped to relax and enjoy some leisurely days with no particular plans.

Curiously, I found no one there at the tiny but official-looking gate house. As the sign requested, I tendered a few Scottish pounds into the narrow slot in the door. Then I began wandering about the lush green grounds, drawn toward a familiar-feeling path.

Below the castle, I discovered an abandoned mooring that once led out to the tides of the River Tay. It is a splendid little cove, intimate and overgrown. I sat down to rest my feet and to admire the abundance of nature within this lush and inviting bit of paradise. It felt slightly brooding yet warm and protective.

I happened to notice a small cave-like structure with a low ceiling and a gently sloping floor. There were tumbled-down rocks at the opening where it looked like there had once been a bit of a wall. I sat down, carefully laid back upon the cool refreshing rock, relaxed into its recalcitrant embrace, and started breathing deeply.

Almost immediately, there was an intense cavernous eruption of pain slashing across my shoulder, back, and side. After the wincing and groaning subsided, I became aware of a dying young Scot; confused and delusional, being consumed by the burning fever brought on by putrefied wounds.

But the greatest agony was a sense that there had been a tragically mistaken betrayal that came with such a savage and resolute blow that it had become etched into the lad's very soul; fearing that he had become forever misunderstood with no opportunity for clarification or redemption.

After a few minutes which seemed to go on for a fortnight, I climbed back toward the castle with a heaviness that felt like the doom of the forgotten dead. I meandered into the beckoning castle which had either a missing or unlocked door, wandered about the main hall, and stood before the great hearth that once sported an ornate and authoritative looking mantle.

In my mind's eye I soon became aware of a wise and gentle presence of a very weary soul. He stood before me in full Highland garb and looked upon me with a kindness that I have seldom known. He bade me welcome. It seemed that he had decided to kneel and was beginning to pray. So I knelt and prayed with him as our souls intermingled. Then, there came a long, uplifting and joyful sigh.

This was Malcolm who had followed Colin into the spirit realm to the foot of Elcho, hoping to make contact, so that both might be liberated from their tragic burden. Malcolm remained, waiting for his friend and young protégé within the castle Elcho for the ensuing generations.

It became a place that was a sort of halfway house, between this world, the spirit realms, and the heavenly dimensions beyond. He would attract lost and confused spirits unto himself and minister unto them until they were able to slip their earthly ties and move on to their next planes of existence.

The soul of Malcom seemed to be caught in an eternity of unrelenting penitence, through serving the needs of many lost or halted souls, in the process of releasing the turmoil and traumas that kept them bound to the earthly domain.

Although he had been mentor and shepherd for many, his guilt and remorse continued to cling to him like a heavy shroud of despair. He was kind, insightful, and sympathetic; but deep inside he had remained a very tired, anguished, and tortured soul.

There was the emergence of a primal recognition, of respect and friendship between us; we were guided by a great soulful presence that cleared our minds, calmed our emotions and fed our souls.

Remembering the pure silver Celtic cross around my neck, I held it before him and his attention was rallied to it. A greater force than I was offering it to him. It was a reminder of the acceptance, the boundless forgiveness and saving grace to be found in an elder brother who had led the way, prepared the path, and opened the door for any who would follow.

The Holy Presence grew strong around us; it was between us and most assuredly within us. There was at that moment a definitive, undeniable dawning—a realization that Colin and I were one.

Once again, I had found myself walking between the rain drops into another a time and place where the revealing and the healing could begin.

Colin and Malcom embraced for the longest time; the kind of embrace that can only come between an adoring son and a loving father. The light permeated everywhere and within everything, releasing all that was ready and needing to be released. Then, like a wisp of a shadow, he vanished and was gone. I remained there for a while, enshrouded by the all-pervading presence.

I don't remember much after that. I found myself in Perth, near the city center; I was walking along the river, across the parade grounds of that historic and legendary regiment called the Black Watch.

Sometimes, for a moment, I can feel Malcom. He may come at a troubling time, with a fond greeting or an uplifting message. I think mostly, he just wants to once again acknowledge the joy of the presence we now share together.

Ever since that encounter, on that warm August afternoon. I simply refer to the Castle at Elcho as Malcom's Castle.

Chapter Four

The Call of Scotland

Three days before her physical transition, my wife had encouraged me to consider visiting Scotland; suggesting that there, I might well find the portal of the next phase of my life. This message had not come from her but through her; from that familiar channeled presence that we casually referred to as the Source.

It always feels like I am going home when I return to Scotland. There is something there that stirs my blood. There are places where these eyes have never been yet are drawn to starkly familiar scenes as I begin to remember. Often images and sounds emerge; being recalled as if from a deep dreaming state where they refuse to remain buried in the subconscious of the past.

Scotland is a place where I shall always belong. No one will ever be able to tell me anything different. Perhaps it is an echo from my soul's sojourn in another age; or, perhaps something resonating, absorbed deeply within the DNA of this subsequent flesh body that recognizes other times and places.

My Grandfather would offer a wide variety of favorite sayings, sounding simplistic and trite at times; yet at second glance often held a lifetime of experience and wisdom. As the years meander along, I become more and more enamored of him.

One such saying was, "You'll never learn any younger." As I heard the call of the highland pipes, I yearned to be able to play at least three or four simple tunes. However, I was in my mid-fifties and taking on such a time-consuming endeavor, so late in life, seemed quite foolish—beyond a reasonable person's grasp.

With the constant encouragement, if not the outright nagging of my wife, I had finally decided to at least look into it. Her incessant reminder of the Grandfather's admonition, "You'll never learn any younger," became the foundation of her conviction. Later it was suggested by her Source that, "This activity could serve you well." There were no more excuses. So I responded and moved forward.

Bagpipes are a very special and sacred instrument; it is an ancient instrument spawned by a progression of various flutes, whistles, and drones tied into different sizes and shapes of bags, usually crafted from the skin of an animal. There was a long, relentless evolution, a quest for something unusual and powerful. The earliest contraptions made their way through the Middle East and Northern Africa, carried by Roman Legions onto Britain's shores during campaigns of conquest and occupation. Caesar's minions were held behind the wall; a wall of their own construction, thereby acknowledging that what lay to the north did not belong to them; it was beyond their capacity to subdue.

In Scotland, the Highland Bagpipe was perfected and imbued with mystical authority and a soul. In the hands of an anointed piper the instrument becomes a tool of spiritual power that can connect Scotland's sons and daughters to other times and places; and even to other worlds.

There is nothing else like it. I have always suspected that those who do not resonate with the many moods of the glorious halcyon cry of the pipes have most likely come from the anguished bloodline of those ancestors, who for hundreds of years strove so unsuccessfully to crush the Highland Spirit.

It is such a formidable instrument that the English, fearing it, once banned it; declaring it an instrument of war. When revived, it often led Scottish soldiers into the vanguard of battle; clearing the way for the rise of an empire called Britain.

I am so grateful to my friend and mentor Hugh E. Thackaberry, an American Scot from Glasgow, whose patience and convictions afforded me the opportunity to become a piper. He was a Warrior of the Korean Conflict. He was a Pipe Major with a most magnificent heart; possibly the most outspoken, cantankerous, and yet loving man I have ever known. He will be with me forevermore.

I became a convener and regional representative of our ancestral clan in Ayershire, Scotland. I involved myself in many Scottish festivals and gatherings across the American West; participated in parades and received several awards on behalf of my Clan for occasionally being the best at something.

Three times I was selected to be part of a committee, judging the Clans in the annual parade down the main street in Estes Park, Colorado. It was kind of like joining the circus.

There was a whole community of like-minded clan folk that would travel far, set up their clan booths, greet friends, participate in activities; and then tear down and meet again in few weeks, or months, at the next location, over and over again. It became like one huge migrating family, providing a special kind of kinship and recognition that is treasured and honored to this day.

I became a proud owner of three kilts and had traditional Scottish attire fit for any occasion. Somehow, I even managed to receive two medals for my piping in regional competition. Yes, I claimed my roots as an American Scot and my son proudly displays the tattoo of his Clan's Crest Badge on his left shoulder. It is good to know who you are and where you come from, in this world as well as in the next.

In preparation for my first sojourn into Scotland, I had asked my Scottish-born piping teacher for some suggestions about where I should go and what I should see. After about an hour's discussion I began to realize that "Hughy," as we affectionately called him, was taking me around his homeland in a great circle. He would tell me one story after another of the many great adventures he had enjoyed.

I realized he was taking me across the country from one pub to another. When I brought this to his attention, a confused and surprised look came upon his face. Then he grinned and roared with laughter, as he realized that those recollections were from his drinking days. And, maybe, that's all he remembered of those particular times and places.

But I took from him the idea of picking a handful of places, with a route spreading as if in a horse shoe or rainbow; starting from the west of Scotland in Glasgow, north through the Highlands, then down the east coast to Edinburgh and back to Glasgow once more.

For me, it was purely an earthly paradise. I have never liked cities; but the cities in Scotland, or at least the ones I visited, were like walking through living hystory. They felt friendly, cozy and alive; full of sights, sounds, ways of living that even now bring a radiance and contentment to my heart and soul. It was a joy to wander through the streets; visit and feel the countless legends of struggle, intrigue, and adventure.

I walked through the greens in the town of Peebles, a place once recalled by my grandfather as he half sang and half hummed a little ditty he said that he had learned from his grandfather. Now, I sometimes strut through a gathering at the grounds of a festival sporting a Scottish kilt made from tartan designed by the Hunter cousins in Peebleshire.

During my travels, I once felt myself dashing through the entry of a great cathedral; cape fluttering, with great fury and passion, accompanied by the rapid clattering of hollow sounding footsteps beating across worn paving stones of a floor that was hundreds of years old.

I stood upon the ramparts of castle fortifications embracing the turmoil, the pride, the despair; the stark terror of clashes both devastating and triumphant.

I stood upon rocky cliffs that bore witness to swarms of Viking invaders, with traditions and deeds, courageous and glorious; as well as brutal and tragic; brought to the isles in square-sailed, wooden boats, bounding upon relentless waves toward conquest and destiny.

I wandered across the rich pagan soil of an ancient Eden that gave birth to a hundred generations; yearning, growing, producing legends and miracles; igniting an enlightenment that spread westward into the promise of an emerging New World.

I fell to my knees on ancient battlefields at Selkirk, Flodden, Sterling Bridge, Bannockburn, and Culloden where my ancestors cast their last ounce of courage against a common foe in order to preserve a sovereign way of life—to protect home and family and clan.

I clung to narrow winding stairs, climbing to the top of the Brave Heart Monument; built by Carnegie, a Scottish son returning home from his triumphs in America. There, I looked over the lush green countryside, where the river wound through a mystical crucible, fruitful in both hystory and fable. I gazed across the valley at stately Stirling Castle, once called Snowden, where some are coming to believe that the legend of King Arthur had begun.

I lumbered up the slopes of Ben Nevis, past the lakes, into the fog, and across the escarpment of crags to the pinnacle; the highest point in all of Scotland, and of all Britain too, for that matter.

There I nestled into the tiny stone structure and added my prayer feathers among the flags of many nations. I shared passage with an old soul, lost from another time; meandering through the mysts of his own unfolding journey. I embraced a wildly pagan, red-headed Goddess, who walked with me between the raindrops and poured peace and contentment into my thirsting Scottish soul, and bade me to come find her once more.

I sat within the sanctity and mystery of Rosalyn Chapel and pondered the ramifications of the many secrets and esoteric teachings hidden in plain sight. I touched Hiram's Pillar and sat where I had sat before. I walked down Merlyn's path and recalled how to remember and live backwards.

In Edinburgh gazing from my hotel room window at the Waverly, I was captivated by the grandeur and cleverness of the Scot Monument. I drank from it deeply, with much humility and gratitude for a nation's appreciation of one so dedicated to the preservation and advancement of Scotland's heritage and traditions.

Among my favorite places in Scotland is the Sacred Isle of Iona in the Inner Hebrides. It is a place where the veil between this world and the next is thin and magic can happen. I hope to return there once again before this life becomes complete.

To get there, you travel northwest from Glasgow to Oban and take the ferry to the Isle of Mull at Craignure. From that point there is a westward journey of some 12 miles along a narrow, shoulderless, one-lane road. It can be sufficient to make the weak-hearted a little squeamish when the sparse local traffic is met, sprinting towards you from the opposite direction.

There is grass so green, thick, and abundant that it would be a cattleman's paradise; or shepherd's if you prefer. There are a few marshes with standing water and an occasional outbreak of small stands of trees such as ash, oak, birch, and willow. There are craggy knolls thrown in for good measure; mostly located along rocky shores. And, there are standing stones whose origin and purpose have been lost to legend and mystery.

At the end of this road, which in places is barely more than a path, is the community of Fionnphort. There, determined people cling to life and traditions as ancient as Scotland herself. There are a couple of small houses converted into restaurants where food and drink is simple and incredibly satisfying.

There are several bed and breakfast establishments. They are small; not ostentatious. I have not been there for a while so by now commercial tourism is probably changing the community and its landscape.

From Fionnphort you can look across the waves to timeless Iona. It is an island that measures barely one by three miles. There, in 563 CE, Saint Columba settled and built an Abbey. This was the Holy Man who was exiled from Ireland and credited with bringing Christianity to the Isles. Iona became a destination for pilgrimage. This was the place where Colin had been, under the sponsorship of Malcolm.

During the darkest ages in Europe this was a place where learning and hystory were sequestered, treasured and kept alive. The many Lords of Argyll are credited with the protection and support of the Abbey during disparaging and turbulent times.

They had once colluded with the Jacobite cause, to keep Scotland free and independent.

There in Iona, in a modest graveyard, is the secluded and isolated burial place of close to 50 medieval kings. Not far away still stands a primitive little chapel where great sagas, legends, and ballads were born and honored. The little complex of buildings from the original monastery lays somewhat in ruins.

The current Abbey and Cathedral at Iona was built by the Viking, Raghnall, around 1200. It now serves a surviving Benedictine Community of worshipers. In the tradition of standing stones, there are many Celtic crosses across the island, but the largest and most impressive ones seem to be located around the current abbey. I have touched some that were close to twelve feet tall; complete with ancient, pagan, Celtic carvings deeply engraved upon them.

Archaeologists have removed and gathered up many of the stones and placed them in a room behind the cathedral, supposedly in an effort to protect them from further weathering and deterioration.

On my first pilgrimage to Iona I brought three, small, clear crystals from the mountains in Colorado, and I planted them there in the rich sandy soil, beneath an enormous Celtic cross. They were placed as an offering and blessing from the sacred valley in the San Juan Mountains.

There are almost no vehicles on the island; only vehicles that provide essential services and supplies. They are floated across the several hundred yards on a ferry that would be unable to handle more than four or five vehicles. The ferry arrives at a little port where a modest avenue of shops and honored ancestral homes provide for the basic needs of visitors. There is public lodging on the island, but it is sometimes hard to secure.

Though it only takes 10 or 15 minutes, it is a crossing into an ancient time, from whence came the solidification of the new age of Celtic culture and tradition, moving into and across our modern world. In some minds, it has evolved to a point where it is giving way to an even newer way of seeing and believing; which may be in part a revival of the old ways seen with new eyes.

Chapter Five

Dulcinea in Iona

On my last trip to Iona I brought a companion. I had met her in an historic western town at a cowboy poetry gathering. When first we met, it seemed we were instantaneously melded together with an intensity that, for me, was both primal and terrifying. It was as if we had always been an inseparable part of each other. I was as the proverbial moth, drawn to the flickering flame.

It was not uncommon to feel her presence before she would arrive. Though hundreds of miles apart, there were times when I could feel her right next to me. I could feel her breath, and the warmth of her body lying beside me. Several times, I was startled, shaken, when I would turn and discover that she was not actually there, at least not physically. Often I could accurately sense what she was thinking and feeling when we were far apart. And it was the same for her.

Among the things discovered was that, although unknown to each other, we had spontaneously, and independently acquired and were listening to the same music, at the same time; though we might not have seen each other for weeks. There was scarcely an esoteric construct or a spiritual path that we had not independently explored and shared.

It used to make me feel a bit uneasy to admit it, but now after the passage of time, I can truthfully say that our merging was even stronger; more consistent and more intimate than the one

I had originally experienced with my deceased wife, my blessed Susan.

It is most likely that this new lady was indeed intended to become what the romantics like to call "the love of my life."

And as the poet once wrote:

> "I was lost in her eyes and adored her long hair; I'd never seen a mature woman so fair. She was a powerful woman full of wisdom and grace. If you want to know God; just look in her face ..."

We had made our pilgrimage during the Gathering of the Clans in Edinburgh in 2009. It was ostensibly a national celebration, a formal welcoming home for all of Scotland's scattered sons and daughters.

I introduced my Lady to my Clan Chief, and 30th Laird of Hunterston. We stood together on the ramparts of the castle's pele tower, on land where my Chief's family had endured for over 900 years. We watched and participated in the celebration where clan folk had assembled from all over the world; brought together by one common heritage. We celebrated with the pipers, the dancers, and the archers. We were seated next to our Chief at her banquet. It was an event both solemn and joyful.

Later at Edinburgh Castle, we strode down the cobblestone streets to and through the grounds of Holyrood Palace; currently occupied by an English prince with stolen Scottish titles. (But I am not political; I have no thoughts on the subject.) We paraded together, with our banners flying, with all the rest of the Scottish Clans. Hearts were full of passion, pride, and fire; and we rejoiced.

During our tour, my Lady and I visited a variety of both popular and seldom trod places of interest. Now, we were proceeding to this sacred and revered Isle whose original Gaelic name translates to the *"Isle of the Druids."* This was the place where, in modern times, the ancient pagan ways merged with something called Christianity and birthed a newer version of Celtic heritage and culture.

I have always cherished and revered the Celtic cross. To me, its pagan circle, wrapped around the center of the cross, represents and symbolizes the blending of the wisdom and power of both traditions.

Right there, in the mydst of the new beginning is the eye of Wodan, the Alfather, merged with the cross. What part of the name—All Father—do we not understand? The Father of All, uniting with the symbol of the Resurrected Christ. Yes, I know some of those old Nordic and Celtic practices could be quite cruel and barbarous; but then again so were some of those early Christian atrocities, as those movements grew out of their infancy.

The Celtic cross brings to my mind, not the creation of a new, dominating force to crush and obliterate the old ways, but rather a Messianic force to heal and unite; sanctify and complete. Christ coming to fulfill; not to destroy.

The previous day we had hiked through the heather upon spongy, moss-covered ground, and danced among boulders and ancient standing stones that overlooked the sea.

We meditated together and watched a crimson sun settle into a golden ocean from whence came a gentle, playful breeze, full of feathered beings; gliding, diving among the primeval craggy cliffs; where wanton waves relentlessly pounded and retreated in breathless, undulating ecstasy. We touched and embraced the vortex of all creation.

We teased and laughed like children and held each other; close. We drank deeply of this special place. Now our crossing was upon the horizon; and we drifted toward the beckoning adventure.

Up near the bridge, I gazed upon the goddess-like visage of my extraordinary companion. She was searching, excitedly with great curiosity, toward the approaching shore. Her long, auburn hair fluttering and dancing around her head and shoulders; then settling gracefully across her back. Her spirit beckoned to me and I rejoiced, engraving the perfect moment deep within my heart; where it lingers still.

I was leaning against the stout iron railing that wrapped around the upper passenger deck of the ferry. In my pocket, I was fondling the ring belonging to my beloved Susan and thinking about our life together and wondering about what would come next.

I had a bit of a ritual in mind. I was leaving one shore and heading straight into the next. I formed a silent prayer and casually released her ring into the mysteries of the swirling, dark blue, Ionian waters.

Susan was with me and in agreement. She seemed to like the metaphor and gave me her blessing. It was a way of releasing; moving on, as they say.

As my Lady and I set foot upon holy ground we were mostly quiet—taking in the moment. We walked past the shops and up around the modern buildings toward the still stately ruins; ancient burial mounds and gardens that lay along the path. Treasuring our own private thoughts and feelings, we wandered around the sacred grounds, savoring that which was ours to savor.

We looked into the tiny, crumbling chapel where apostles of Erin once prayed, and kings were affirmed and eulogized. But, as I stepped inside, I felt a nauseating chill and could swear I heard moaning.

We passed by the iconic MacLean's Cross that has greeted so many pilgrims over the centuries. Soon we were standing at the threshold of the Iona Abbey Church, that to me has as much grandeur as any cathedral. But, it is not large and overpowering like many a traditional cathedral. This is sanctified ground, and no earthly bishop can rule over it.

When you step inside, you find yourself standing upon huge, flat stones that form a platform that looks down into the nave where parishioners would sit. It is basically a simple elongated design with traditional wings at the intersection. It has an exceptionally high, but typical, vaulted ceiling supported by Gothic-like, stone arches. The ceiling is made from and is braced by thick, hand-hewn timbers.

Though primitive in style, still it offers an appearance that, to my mind, was surprisingly ornate. It harkens back to the look and feel of the great halls of the Norsemen.

As you step down, and move toward the raised altar at the other end of the nave, you become aware of areas along the side aisles which could be used as choir lofts. Of course, there are also the customary areas, where there are niches for shrines, and a larger space where established rituals and gatherings can be conducted. From the wings, there is access to the cloisters and the inner sanctum of the abbey itself.

There are places where effigies of heroes and benefactors reside, along with an exquisitely carved marble sarcophagus of some high born who are revered because they once defended and supported the abbey.

We sat separately and meditated a while, allowing ourselves to take in the enormous richness of the time and place in which we found ourselves. I found my own inner presence wafting up, within and around me; my constant companion, the one He called the Comforter.

In my mind, I began to carefully recite the poem I had laboriously crafted. It was prepared long before the advent of the pilgrimage and our journey taken together. She, was seated somewhere along the nave; I, along the wings. I began to feel her: her mind, her heart, her soul. I beckoned to her in my spirit.

"Can you hear me; can you feel me; will you give me your attention; will you come to me?" This was what I was saying and asking of her.

After a moment she abruptly looked up, scanning the gallery alongside the wing where I sat. Our eyes locked—so did our thoughts and minds; two souls converging as one. I rose, walking slowly, deliberately, around the pillars and down into the aisle.

Her eyes were intent and focused; she watched me closely to see where I was going. I walked to the altar, standing straight and tall, upon the platform. I lingered there, upon the sanctuary.

I gestured for her to come to me. She looked a little surprised and suspicious. Again, I bid her to come to me. She resisted and I asked again. She held her ground.

I began to move toward her and my guardian spirit erupted saying,

"No, allow her to come to you."

Once more, I motioned to her. She stood resolute. Her tender gaze became an inquisitive hardened stare. After a moment she quickly moved to the back of the church and stepped up on the high platform at the vestibule, where we had entered. She stood motionlessly, looking back toward me; where I was still positioned, upon the altar.

In her spirit, she was defiant,

"No, you come to me," was her answer.

Her countenance became demanding, commanding. I decided to go to her. From the well of my being came the admonition, once again.

"No, she must come to you!" This time it was stronger and sternly offered.

We stood watching each other for what seemed like several minutes. Then, against the better advice; I went to her, as she stood upon the platform at the back of the church.

She seemed amused and smiled with what seemed like both triumph and accusation. I croaked out my little poetic rendition of the ancient Celtic ritual; acknowledging, proclaiming, and seeking the advent of our assumed betrothal, and impending union.

Looking at me blankly, she quipped,

"That's the dumbest thing I ever heard."

She turned and left the building immediately; said she was not feeling well and wanted to go back, because her stomach was hurting. There was nothing she wanted to discuss.

The energy totally shifted and had changed. She decided to get something to drink and to go sit somewhere. Everything felt awkward and at odds.

The ferry was not coming back for at least a couple of hours, so I took the long walk to visit the Druid ruins on the other side of the island. I thought of approaching her again; perhaps she did not understand my clumsy intention.

From the depths of my being erupted, "No! You must not do this; do not submit to this!"

Later, as if clarifying, the Source came to me and intoned, "It is for the bride to be brought to the groom at the altar; not for the groom to be brought to the bride."

I pondered that perspective for many months without achieving sufficient confidence in my understanding. I can make up possibilities and probabilities, but never have I quite understood with certainty what transpired on the enchanted isle.

That which could not be broken. Was broken. It was done in a way and at a place that may never be grasped with my limited, finite reasoning; perhaps I don't need to …

She was not to become "bone of my bone and flesh of my flesh" as the ancient proto-ritual proclaims.

Later on we attempted, several times, to recover that which was lost, but to no avail.

Always did it seem she would be found flirting; seeking a better deal, even in front of me. She too was drawn like a moth to the flame; a flame of better, more interesting, more fun, more powerful and affluent people.

Once started, she would often not stop drinking until she could no longer stand, or had slipped into stupor. She would travel great distances at a whim, with people she barely knew; without adequate finances, with no particular plan or concern for outcomes. She always seemed short of money. She moved on into other arms, often.

Together we had experienced great joy and passion. We really had a good time. And we also brought great tragedy and sorrow to ourselves, through a connection and a purpose we apparently did not adequately comprehend or agree upon.

I am sure that in the end she has her own special recollections; her own story to treasure. We learned much on our pilgrimage together. Through the travail remains my conviction that, in the end, all will be made glorious. I so cherished my beloved Dulcinea.

She helped me to remember, recover, and understand that more satisfying, eternal place; where I could find an ever-enduring love and acceptance; that for so long my heart had been craving, my soul had been seeking; to not look for love in the wrong places.

All is well.

Later, returning to the mainland, I wandered about the majestic ruins of the Abbey in Melrose where the brave heart of Wallace, the father of Scotland, is buried.

Returning home for a few days at Abbotsford House, I sat beside my beloved river, Tweed; and recalled better times.

I gazed upon all the special little artifacts; the favored collections of things gathered from travels into the heritage and hystory of the legendary Scottish saga. I touched the desk where Scott wrote his many inventive and inspired stories.

Looking at what was touted as his favorite chair; well that wasn't the favorite. The curator got it wrong. That's where he would lay supported upright, gazing out the window wrapped in his blankets, with his dogs around him; offering him comfort, as he ruminated and coalesced about the finances necessary to support his always evolving, never-ending projects.

We hobble down the path beneath the trees to the dilapidated stables that some mistakenly believe was once the Abbot's residence, for whom the house received its name. I wonder if they know about the hidden passages and the ceremonial chambers where spirit still thrives.

Though he warily denied it in public; cultural historians might be surprised to discover some of the arcane knowledge and secrets he practiced there, inspired by the Templars.

I find myself lost in remembering, as I kneel beside the statue in the garden—here he is down on one knee, hands folded in prayer, looking toward the heavens. Yes, dear friend, we were great once; but what have we done lately.

Spirit whispers: *"Stand still too long; wisp of a shadow and you are gone ... ."*

It was time for the Wizard of the North to return to America; to live in this life and not so much in the past.

Chapter Six

Punchin' Cattle

There's a national park down in southcentral Utah called Capitol Reef where tourists like to stop and admire the Gifford Homestead. It's a place where a pioneering Mormon community once flourished. It even had a small, one-room school house. Most of the buildings are preserved; the orchards are still productive. It's sort of a living museum. It's an isolated place that prospered because it has water; an oasis in the middle of what some say is a desolate and barren land.

I swear the sweetest cherries I've ever tasted are grown right there in the bottom of that little ravine. It's wedged within a red rock canyon with cottonwood trees and a few pastures with fairly good grass.

There is what they call a "water fold" that runs through the area for several miles. This geologic feature is like a big wrinkle in the crust of the earth—trapping water and creating ridges and canyons where ancient hunter-gatherers once thrived.

Now there is a campground, with a batch of park rangers who tell you where to go, what happened there, how to think about it. Most of the surrounding area is a national park. There are a lot of popular nature trails. Some follow the old routes and cover great distances. These were mostly established by early explorers, following in the footsteps of Freemont Indians. However I don't believe any of those people ever called themselves by that name.

There are places where so called "First Peoples" left their mark along the canyon trails. Along one wall, you can see where the later explorers and pioneers also left a record; carving their names with dates and sometimes messages. It was as a sort of bulletin board and rallying point for groups that would follow, as well as a monument to the success of the earlier expeditions.

Though it is all civilized now, it can still be a dangerous place. Don't go anywhere without water. Searing summer heat, sometimes reaching well over one hundred degrees, can induce exhaustion and heat stroke. Flash floods can trap and kill if you get caught in the wrong place. If you see clouds, even far away, it's best to keep your eyes open, and your ears listening for rushing water.

I was summoned to help move cattle on the back side of this little haven; a place that the moderns call, Capitol Reef.

Much of the ranch is fairly barren, almost Middle-Eastern looking. The route from the east is about twenty miles over gravel and dirt roads. Sometimes a road gets washed out.

The desert gets only a few inches of precipitation a year. And this year the droughts weren't helping much. Only one small stream, on the western side of the ranch, provides any opportunity to grow grass and raise cattle. The stream is carefully engineered to bring water down from the rain- and snow-catching mesas, toward the west. Perhaps the ranch's most valuable financial asset is the government leases it holds along the modest mountain ranges where grass, brush and trees flourish.

Some cattlemen were developing a special strain of cattle; fit for a market interested in non-feed-lot, grass-fed beef. It was an experimental project that had grown into breeding stock of about five hundred head. The ranch manager has plans to build a larger herd that he is sure can be financially sustainable.

He has disagreements with corporate owners who live in Pennsylvania and visit once a year to keep an eye on their investment. Previously, he had been forced to sell off two-thirds of the stock to raise money to make the books balance. He had hoped that building and keeping a larger herd would offer more to harvest, year after year. Otherwise, it's kind of like selling too much of your wheat. Then you are short of seed to plant for a full crop the next year.

Except for improvements to the main ranch cabin, the remote operation looked like something out of an Old West movie set. Running water had been established. There was an inadequate solar generator with components sequestered in a small building with an uneven roof that sagged and needed repair. Batteries didn't hold charges very well, and lights didn't last long. The paddock and out buildings were functional and in adequate condition. They had an appearance of being rather antique or historic; not of this modern age.

Most of the five or six buildings looked like original log structures with some partially covered with adobe. One was obviously a bunk house. Another had a floor raised high, as if providing a loading dock for the small warehouse.

Scant fencing looked like it came from felled trees up on the mesa, a long, long time ago.

I originally made contact with the outfit by hobnobbing with some cowboy-poet buddies, and asking a lot of questions. Cows and young calves needed to be driven up along the mesas into the high, squatty-green mountain ranges for summer grazing.

It was my impression that this was only one of several smaller operations that the "ranch boss," as he was called, was managing. He was like a working overseer with a sort of assisting caretaker who was living on the premises. One was named Bret, the other Adam. Adam seemed happy to have some help. Bret didn't seem too sure.

This was my first real cowboy "gig."

They were looking for a temporary, extra hand. Though willing to take a chance on me, I'm sure I wasn't their first choice. After some cordial introductions, I was assigned one of the two bunks in a room where remodeling was just completed. The smell of drying paint and green lumber was still lingering; outgassing as they say.

I was abruptly taken to one of the buildings near the paddock to select a "proper" saddle. It was assumed I didn't have one.

This abandoned old tack shed left me swimming in a sea of sensations and impressions of days long ago.

It was full of rusting, antiquated tools and old saddles. Harness and tack was encrusted with a thick patina of moldering dust, and was severely cracking. There were no windows. However, there where sections where random rays of daylight streamed through crumbling calking made from caliche-clay. There was the smell of rotting mice.

It was obvious that there had been a much larger operation that had withered over time and almost slipped away. I was wondering if cleaning out this tack room might become one of my duties.

I dragged an old roping saddle out of the darkness and fumbled with an inadequate, antique hackamore bridal, but decided I would use the snaffle that I brought with me.

Then I was then asked one, very pointed, direct question.

"Well, have you ever been on a horse?"

Fortunately, I had. But I was a long way from what anyone might consider to be an accomplished horseman. I responded that I was greener than green but a remarkably fast learner. I think I lied on both accounts.

Straight away, from out of a sparse remuda, I was assigned my pony, Jeremiah, an old campaigner. When I fed him, I offered him some horse treats; horse cookies some like to call them. He stared at me blankly. He let them fall out of his mouth.

I don't think he had ever seen such a thing. Didn't know what they were. I acknowledged that he was not a pet or playmate. Though we might become respectful partners, Jeremiah was a serious professional, a working horse.

Adam and I were paired together. He seemed relieved at the prospect of having some help. Ranch Boss Bret disappeared; supposedly driving the long way around with a horse trailer. He planned to meet us at a water tank, near some halfway place in the late afternoon. There was mention that he was headed over toward Torrey to handle some other ranch-related business.

Later, I observed that there were an additional couple of hands, hauling water and tending to other tasks that were mostly somewhere beyond the horizon. They sometimes showed up at meal time, looking like they had stepped out of another era, two or three generations from the past.

The food was well-prepared and plentiful. We carried noon-time snacks in saddlebags. Sometimes we made our own break-fast. We were supplied with a talented and capable cook who would come and go, obviously tending to other errands.

Bret would sit at the head of the table. He would not tolerate anyone having a hat on while seated at the table. He considered it an insult to the cook—his wife. He presented as a serious, sullen man of few words who could nevertheless enjoy a good joke. He was fair, but all business. You would not want to cross him. He was the boss. He expected you to know your cowboy eti-quette. His horse got watered first. Everything started at sunup. Everything stopped at sundown.

Adam was friendly and talkative. I found most of his spiel to be quite helpful. I guess it was part of his job to get me to a place where I understood what was going on; what role I was to play. He was a young man fumbling with an early cell phone with almost no reception, trying to keep informed. We could commu-nicate with handheld radios, but to function properly they had to be mostly in line-of-sight, and at short distance.

We followed a stream for about two miles toward the mesa where the occasional moaning and bellowing of cattle could be heard. We began to encounter tall grass along with a few willows and aspen. The source of the stream was a patch of wetlands that looked like it was fed by springs, draining from the escarp-ment a couple thousand feet higher.

This is where the herd had been left to wander. They had spread out in all directions. Very expensive, breeding cattle; mostly moms along with their young calves. Out there some-where there was a missing bull. We were hoping to locate it as we gathered up the herd. There was concern. Apparently, there had been some talk about modern-day rustlers in the area.

There could be some other cattle in the mix. We didn't need to worry much about that, until fall; just identify them so the ranch boss could let the other outfits know where their stock had wandered off to. Of course you had to get close enough to read the plastic ear tag, fortunately they were color-coded as well as numbered. It was a gentlemen's agreement. They did the same for us. It was basically open range, except for the dictates of the Bureau of Land Management.

The task was to gather and push them up and around a long steep ridge to the flatter ground in the high country where they could feed and mature through the summer. It was a tough, hard climb. Some of the older matrons of the herd did not want to go. They would rather linger around the tall green grass and plentiful water at the bottom of the mesa.

As instructed, I nudged Jeremiah into a fast trot and moved methodically in an arc around and toward the left, while Adam took up the right flank. After some resistance and a few games of "peak-a-boo" around the willows, we began to dislodge and form up the herd. They complained loudly as they began their slow, lumbering climb upward, toward the greener grass on the mesa.

It soon became clear that there were some deserters along the way. Some would hide among the tall thick oak brush and hope we would pass them by, while others would move out front, out of view; then circle back down the mountain ridges, to go back to where we started.

A bunch started to break out on the right flank, heading out through the trees and back down toward the plain below. Adam spurred his horse and lunged over the edge of the ridge. He had been fussing with that horse all morning. Several times he had to move away from the herd and put the horse through its paces; riding in tight circles and figure eights, fast starts; quick, sliding stops; with a lot of spur.

It was his own personal mount. He said he paid over twenty-thousand dollars for it. He was looking toward competitive rodeo and wanted to use him for calf roping and steer wrestling events.

I weren't no expert, but I had to admit it was a gorgeous looking hunk of horse flesh. It was black, sleek and shiny. I judged it to be about eighteen hands high. He seemed to be anxious and nervous all the time; often throwing his head and prancing.

It was obvious he had a lot of power and stamina. It was what they liked to call a "spirited" horse.

As the ballads say "he had fire in his eyes." Two or three times, I spotted the horse galloping over the uneven ground at full speed, dogging trees and small boulders, rider expertly clinging to a bouncing, swerving saddle, hunched low with high elbows and flapping reins.

I was not sure if Adam was chasing a cow or simply trying to get his runaway horse back under control. After a while, horse and rider would circle back and once more Adam would start putting his rambunctious steed through his paces. I think it was part showing off, and part fighting for control—so he could get back to "punching cattle."

The animal was supposedly from the Joe Hancock blood line. In some circles these horses are highly valued. Adam described the horse as fast and spirited and the perfect partner for his rodeo dreams.

The truth is, I have never quite understood the value of a "spirited horse." To me, they are crazy; skittish, impulsive, unpredictable; mostly, unnecessarily dangerous. Perhaps their riders admire them for their independent and rebellious nature. Perhaps these are wranglers who just need the challenge; always trying to prove their value to themselves. Personally, I have always preferred the Jeremiah's of the remuda; solid, reliable, and responsive. My idea of a good ride has always been: *I don't get hurt; the horse doesn't get hurt; we do our job and get home.*

As Adam once again galloped over the edge and into the abyss, I was beginning to face my own challenges. The herd was slowing, breaking up, meandering. On the left flank, they were lumbering into tall, dense oak brush; several with young calves in tow. I nudged Jeremiah with my boot heels and reined him around and into the brush. One by one, sometimes in twos or threes we retrieved our wayward bovine constituents. Alone, me and my pony relentlessly urged them back toward the intended trail.

Sometimes, I would lead Jeremiah into a thicket in which I suspected there might not be an escape. After several frenzied sorties of chasing and playing tag, I began to feel pain in my legs. My Levi's were getting torn up in the brush. Some of the more serious scratches were bleeding. I checked Jeremiah and he too was beginning to show signs of wear.

For the first time that day, I felt myself breathe and relaxed into the saddle. Jeremiah seemed to notice it too. I began to realize that he'd done this before. All that was needed was to point him in a direction. He was actually better than I was at selecting the route and anticipating the cow's next move. So I sort of selected the battles, and he would move into the breach and rescue the campaign. Sometimes, he would just stop. I first saw this as a sign of rebellion, but later came to understand that this was his way of asking for a different plan.

The truth was, I was making it all too complicated, over controlling. I soon discovered that the most important thing was just to keep them moving. Riding around and behind them, with a few hoots or shouts, gave them incentive to join and keep up with the crowd. When they started to wander, I would just position myself up a ways from the corner, along the flank.

Most of the cows that strayed eventually returned toward the herd, as long as the main body kept moving. Simply angling a little toward them, just a bit, created just the right pressure to get them back in line.

Eventually, I half pushed and half followed about three hundred, out along a flattening part of the escarpment, where an old, dug out, catch-basin served as a watering hole. It was mostly boggy and the water was muddy, but thirsty cows didn't seem to mind.

It dawned on me that I was utterly alone. Out in the middle of nowhere, not knowing where the hell Adam had gone. With the cattle rallied at the water hole, I decided to hold up and take stock of the situation. I made a call on the handheld radio, but heard nothing in return. In a few minutes I heard some crackling static but not much else.

Eventually, I picked up half of a conversation where I could hear Bret, the ranch boss, but not my partner who disappeared from the right flank. Seems that when Adam chased cows down into the ravine, he ended up in loose slide-rock where his horse lost a shoe.

He'd taken a tumble, but both rider and horse were sound. We were to reconnoiter a little ways up the trail. Apparently, he had driven a dozen or so up through the trees and right into "my" herd which resulted in some confusion among the alpha cows who were thinking the route had been changed. That had confounded the momentum, contributing to the unappreciated excursion into the oak thickets.

Bret instructed me to get the herd moving again. He was waiting up on top. Told me to just keep 'em moving and I'd see where to go.

The problem was the cattle didn't want to go. Not only were they content to stay at the mud hole, but they had discovered salt-block remnants. The moaning little herd assembled itself around their prize and was guarding it with great determination. There also seemed to be a bit of contention regarding who was the most worthy of partaking of the welcomed treat.

I drove Jeremiah right into the middle trying to dislodge their stronghold and get them moving again. For the most part, these cantankerous critters just let us pass right through them, while bellowing and moaning their disapproval. As a whole, they remained in place.

At the center, was a core of fat, old mama cows. They would occasionally lick at the salt, savoring it right down to the grass, rocks and mud, where it had crumbled in place.

They stood resolute, guarding their salt. This was a group of huge, formidable, old breeders who were refusing to budge.

It suddenly occurred to me that some were substantially bigger and stronger than Jeremiah and I put together. I remembered the admonition not to get into a fight with a large angry cow. Some could be dangerous, start charging and kicking, capable of taking down both horse and rider.

They stared at me defiantly, mostly holding their ground. I jousted at them waving and hollering. We made some headway, but they would just circle back around, showing absolutely no interest in moving up the steep trail.

I could feel my pony becoming a little apprehensive. I yielded to his experience and wisdom. So, I chose the point of least resistance and moved over to the left flank. We backed off, at first; then slowly moseyed and bobbed along the line, like a Scottish war lord rallying his troops.

I took Jeremiah back and forth across the front edge of the line, moving closer and closer toward the herd. Soon they began to move, and in unison. Unfortunately, they began swinging back and forth as if they were on a fulcrum, like a pin wheel around the hub; or a slow moving propeller, swinging back and forth on the shaft. They just milled around in a circle; as a whole, remaining in the same place.

I would move them on one side and then the other side; while alternatively, the two wings would just keep moving back and forth around the center.

Then, I got angry. Figured, I could move quickly back and forth charging one side and then the other, fast enough that both wings would move together—all at once, in the same, opposite direction—thus creating the momentum to finally get them moving. Jeremiah was responsive and dutiful.

I loped him, back and forth, back and forth; until finally stopping in defeat and exhaustion. I was a bit surprised that I could ride so well. I didn't know I had it in me.

For a few minutes I just sat there; legs out of stirrups, crossed wrists resting on saddle horn, reigns held loosely between my fingers. I became aware of my body, legs, back, torso, and arms; tired and shaking, soaked with sweat. This was hard work.

Still no news on the little plastic handheld radio. I mused a little bit, wondering how John Wayne might address this situation. But it weren't no laughing matter. This was serious business. It was getting late. I was alone; not where I was supposed to be. Both horse and rider were becoming quite fatigued. I was getting low on water.

Then behind me, to the left, came the slow clomping of horse beats. It was Bret. I think he had been watching; hopefully more amused than disgusted.

He said something like, "Let's try it together." Glancing at my torn Levi's, he suggested that next time I might try chaps.

He stationed himself on the right flank; motioned to me to do the same on the left. Then, moving slowly, confidently, in tandem; we edged forward. Along with a yip or two, and an occasional slap on my thigh or leather; the cows, in unison, simply moved forward; gracefully, effortlessly, up and along the broad winding trail.

Bret mentioned that Adam had some more trouble but would be along soon. Within a mile or two, we came to a steep, brown hillside; well-worn from previous years' treks.

Again, he positioned me up along the left flank. I found myself in the "sweet spot;" made a few adjustments as needed; up and down, back and forth; keeping pressure on the strays, so they would not turnback, down, around, or behind the left flank.

Adam appeared, adding pressure form the right. Bret remained on the bottom drag line for a few minutes; then he disappeared as quietly as he had come.

The herd just leisurely bellowed its way to the top, where they were greeted by an abundance of fresh water and plentiful oceans of gently swaying grass.

This was my first day. The adventure had begun.

The next few days were spent looking for the lost, missing wayward ones; finding them, coaxing them up and through the trembling aspen into the cattle "promised land." I will always be grateful to Jeremiah. He was steadfast. He never complained. He made me look good.

Of course, there was other work too: getting irrigation started, taking care of, cleaning up, giving a helping hand.

Sometime later, I found myself eavesdropping. I heard the ranch boss ask, "How's he doing?"

Came the response, "Well, he works hard; follows directions. He doesn't get in the way; and, sometimes he's down right helpful."

Came the conclusion, "Guess he'll fit in."

What a wonderful thing; what a magnificent epitaph, for a greenhorn, an old man, to overhear.

A short distance from the bunkhouse was a monumental cliff face. At Adam's suggestion, I half walked and half crawled up to the overhanging, rose-colored wall. Upon it were a couple dozen names and dates; etchings made by cowboys. Some were over a hundred years old.

I made my mark; carved my name upon the stone.

I was a cowboy … !

Chapter Seven
Wranglin' Horses

I like horses a whole lot better than cattle. Cows 'n steers are mostly slow and lumbering; stubborn critters without much sense. They are almost as bad as sheep. They are bad-mannered and ill-tempered; smell awful and are unnecessarily noisy. But, that does make it easier to find them. And they are good to eat.

Driving horses is considerably different than driving cattle. The truth is you can't really drive them. You need to lead them—from the front. The best wranglers are selected to ride at the head of the herd, mostly selecting themselves. The horses chase after and follow. It's not a place for a novice. Leading them is how you direct them; keep them headed where you want them to go. Depending on how many you're tendin', it's good to have some help on the flanks. It keeps rebels from breakin' off and maybe takin' others with them.

Riders at the rear are on drag. It keeps some pressure on the older, slower, tired horses and provides a view; so you can make sure none wander off or get left behind.

I like to ride what they call the corners. It's not quite as dusty, at least some of the time. Of course, you don't get much dust at any position if you're working in the rain or snow. I have done both. The corners offer a good view of how things are progressing. You can drop back over to the drag, when needed or directed by the top hand. Being at the corner of the flank gives you some responsibility to swing up along the sides to head off or turn back any alphas that may be breaking away. You might be the last opportunity get them turned back before someone has to go chase them.

You really don't want to find yourself in the middle of a herd. A fast moving stream of horses can get worked up and wild. Surging, feeling their primal urges, they may erupt; freely leaping, twisting, bucking, perhaps breaking into a gallop with wind-blown forelocks, manes and tails dancing, as they lunge and charge across the range, trampling anything that gets in the way.

No matter how well-trained your pony, and what a great horseman you think you are, your horse can lose his mind, find his heart; leaving you desperately dangling from your saddle or even abandoned in the dirt, lying beneath the onslaught of flailing hoofs.

Horses can get very attached to one another. Sometimes they get separated in the confusion and fury of the drive. They start screaming, calling for their missing buddies, turning back or running frenzied in the wrong direction; disturbing or agitating their fellow travelers. Some members in the mob may get startled or inspired and chase after a runaway, creating a breakout.

A few years ago I was witness to over a hundred horses breaking loose from a herd of some five hundred. It took close to three hours with most of the best wranglers galloping off to find 'em and bring 'em back. It left us short-handed, we hung on the best we could, and that turned out to be good enough.

One late fall, after the Celtic festival in Estes Park, I found myself at a horse stable where I met an old wrangler who had fallen on hard times. He was working as a "dude wrangler," for tips. He was escorting tourists up and down a series of short, one- to three-hour, well-worn trails for a hands-on touch of the "old West."

It was toward the end of the day, but he still offered to take me out. We were just jogging along, side by side, chatting a bit;

when my startled horse rose up and tried to run. He was in fight-or-flight mode.

This was not normal behavior for an old horse sentenced to a life of servitude in a recreational riding stable. He was obviously freaked out by the appearance of several elk that had strayed into our path. Most likely, the strangest livestock he had ever seen. It was no big deal. With a few firm tugs and a couple of kicks, I got him to circle around, keeping him under control. My comrade and I sat for a while, waiting for the semi-domesticated elk, with the large and scary antlers, to wander past.

I was told about a ranch up toward the northwest of Colorado where there was an annual horse drive that I might enjoy. I didn't know anything about it. But I was immediately fascinated and got myself invited.

When we got back to the paddock, I was introduced to the man who managed the stable; went by the handle of "Kansas." He looked me over carefully and seemed to have some reservation. But, my new buddy convinced him that I had what it takes. I signed on for the drive, which wasn't scheduled until next spring. But that gave me a lot of time to brush up on my horsemanship skills.

In the northwest corner of Colorado near and around what was once called Brown's Hole was a ranch of close to one-hundred-thousand acres. The area has a hystory of being a haven for outlaws like Tom Horn, Butch Cassidy, and the Wild Bunch gang.

As many as six-hundred horses are pastured there each winter. I use the word pastured facetiously. It is a vast landscape. For all practical purposes it is an open range where for half the year horses are left alone to be horses. Some of them get pretty wild, almost feral.

It's a cost-effective approach to winter this large collection of mostly quarter horses that run free and graze undisturbed by modern civilization. They are monitored closely through the cold months and offered grass—hay if it turns out it's a hard winter with not much grass to find.

In the late spring, they are gathered and "driven" about sixty miles toward the southeast to a small ranch of about two-thousand acres called, Sombrero. A drive of 600 horses is a lot cheaper than trucking them.

Over the next couple of months they are examined, wormed, sprayed, given new shoes and matched up with tack adequate to serve them for their summer jobs. They are relentlessly herded, sorted, handled, and ridden to get them back in the habit of saddle and bridle. After a long winter with no human contact, some can be a little challenging. But, ultimately these are working horses. They are expected to pay their own way, or they don't stay.

As the weeks roll on, small groups are trucked to locations all over the west, where they will serve in riding stables, hunting lodges, guided wilderness adventures, and just about anything for which you might want a horse. Some have even been movie stars.

In years gone by, hired wranglers, neighbors, friends, and other volunteers would show up for the annual spring ritual of gathering and driving six- or seven-hundred horses. Of course, come fall these horses also need to find their way back home.

It became more and more of a popular event with people coming from all over to help out. As the years wore on, folks got tired of eating out of saddle bags and sleeping on the ground. Of course, some required more help themselves than what they could offer to others. So eventually, things got "better."

These days, folks pay to participate in the drive. I find that immensely clever and humorous. Trucking six-hundred horses costs a fortune. Again, that's why they are driven. Now, most of the riders pay money for the privilege of moving them. But, the up side is that you get a lot of help and logistical support. If you are like me, this is your idea of great fun.

Guests are provided with some instructional orientation; hands-on chores, two horses, food, shelter, and a handy "porta potty" at each official stop. There is a great barbecue with western entertainment and a buckle for the survivors. It's worth every penny. With continued "improvements" and ever-increasing expectations, the event is well on its way to being a premier "Dude Ranch" affair. However, it still remains moderately rough and authentic. I would recommend you first take stock of your body. If needed, do something on a horse to get in shape, before you mount up on the high prairie.

You will ride twenty to thirty miles each of the last two days, on horses that a week before may have been running wild. These are mostly quarter horses. They will all do the job; or, if you insist, you can get a different one. But your horse will most likely be randomly roped out of the herd on the fly. You get to break it in for the season.

Not everyone completes the drive; gate to gate. After two or three days of bouncing around the ranch at Sombrero, a few will decide that this is beyond what they are willing to attempt. There is no dishonor in it. Such an experience is not for just anyone.

This is not a leisurely ride on the back of a slow-walking, half-asleep horse. There are stops to water and rest your horse, but you will spend much of your day at a fast trot or lope; maybe a little galloping if needed, and if you are up for it. Every year it seems there are some spills; but to the best of my knowledge no one has ever been seriously hurt.

Early on, some folks were incensed, insulted even, about the rough, primitive conditions. I guess they were expecting private rooms, with perhaps a little room service and grooms to bring them their mounts. It was not what they had expected; so they left.

That's was alright with the Sombrero cadre. There are always many others on the waiting list. But if you have the heart and spirit for it, they will professionally, calmly, and cheerfully do everything in their power to keep you safe and help you make the trip; earn your buckle, "Gate to Gate."

I love my personal, gaited ponies, but they don't quite seem to hold up like these traditional western mounts. I would not use my personal horses on this drive. I care about them too much. Don't want to put them in a situation where they might get hurt. Most of the ranch "ponies" ride like jack-hammers.

When I return home to my own mounts, it feels like I am riding the back of a large, graceful cat.

Though not required, it is really useful to have some horse experience. The entire event spreads over about six days. The first time was the hardest. Toward the end, I was riding a bit like baggage. But I clung doggedly to my saddle and the horse somehow got me home. I was exhausted and hurting, but safe and sound; proud and grateful for having been able to participate in such a rare and incredibly moving experience.

So I came back. I participated each year for about ten years. I always finished; I never quit. Not once.

After two years, I was offered an "invitation only" opportunity to rendezvous early, up north, and help with the "gather." It would take anywhere from ten days to two weeks to round up the "free range" horses. They would be escorted some fifteen to eighteen miles to the "south pens" as they were called. It is the southernmost holding area for the gather, but the northernmost tip of the actual drive. Photographers collect there—amateur and professional alike—recording the event for friends, publications, and posterity. To take pictures, of course, the BLM wants you to buy a permit.

This is where the drive begins. But it is already the halfway mark for those who have been rounding up the horses and bringing them south. The guests are brought to this point with their horses. This is where they assemble and embark under the supervision of professional wranglers and their assistants. When the horses are released, they are usually restless, agitated, and thirsty. They are anxious, annoyed, and wild; many attempt to escape back to the freedom of the ranges they have ruled all winter.

It is truly a magnificent spectacle: six hundred horses running for five or six miles until they slow and are stopped at the river for water and a brief rest. It's mostly a good place for inexperienced riders to settle down, relax; to get their bearings and prepare for the next leg of the journey.

When I arrived up north toward Brown's Park, at the gather, I was greeted with a bit of suspicion. I arrived pulling my camper trailer, and was immediately recognized and directed to a spot across from a corral, next to an old bunkhouse.

I was hailed by an iconic old cowboy who probably didn't have a lot of years remaining. In his youth he had been a rodeo performer who got gored by a bull in the arena; a horn right under his chin and straight through into his mouth. It put a new tilt to his jaw line. A few lower teeth were ejected and never replaced. He seemed to enjoy telling the story, sort of for shock value. It was effective.

The guy kept telling me he didn't know where I was going to find electricity. They had strung together some extension cords, but the breakers kept going off. A couple of the lady wranglers had come with their own horses along with their camper-horse trailer accommodations. Apparently, a hair dryer kept disrupting the power supply. Over and over, he demanded to know if I need-ed to use a hair dryer. I still don't know if he was serious, or hav-ing a bit of fun with me.

Eventually, I convinced him that I didn't use hair dryers and I really didn't need to be hooked up to power. At first he eyed me some reproachful; but when he saw the scratches, rubs, and wear on my gear, he seemed to think better of me.

I recall him muttering to himself, something like, "At least it looks like he's spent some time on a horse." He particularly appeared to admire the stains and smell of horse-sweat that per-meated my well-anointed saddle and the personal repairs made to my worn chaps.

A few riders were staying in the small, but modern ranch house. The rest were scattered through a couple of small board-inghouse-like structures; built simply, primitively, but added onto and improved over many decades. Two or three were lodged in an old mobile home that wasn't pretty, but served the purpose quite well. We were close to a hundred miles from anything a city dweller would recognize as civilization.

There was a combination meeting room/mess hall staged inside a barn-like structure with a concrete floor. It was usually used as a shop for vehicle storage and repair and anything else that ranch activities might require. It looked like a building that belonged there, and had been there for a very long time.

The cook was a professional who loved his work, and took it seriously. He was a primary source of communication; had a colorful bulletin board. He was clever, entertaining; knew how to listen as well as motivate. He had the bearing and efficiency of an army first sergeant. You could trust him. He was appreciated and respected.

There was variety. No one ever need be hungry. He was well organized, and well supplied; unloaded his whole kitchen from a horse trailer, complete with pantry and refrigeration. Was sort of a modern version of a chuck wagon—still portable, but a whole lot bigger.

An owner and the man in charge, Bishop, talked with me briefly; sort of interviewing me, explaining the routine and assignments, wanting to know if there were questions. He and his wife were both wonderful, capable and easy to talk to, and always had useful answers.

But this was a different kind of camp. You were expected to know what to do, how to handle yourself and take care of business. In the evenings, there was time for fun: playful games, a bit of teasing, wrestling and bedlam; unique traditions suited to the occasion.

The next morning I was put to work. My horse was beautiful. She was branded with the number 2711. Sombrero gave each a horse a number so they could be more easily tracked. The hystory of each horse can be efficiently identified and followed on computer.

Though only 16 or 17 hands high, she was a strong, stocky animal, big-boned; white hair coming through the reddish brown. I wouldn't exactly call her a strawberry roan. Her mane and tail were a lighter color, almost blond. I groomed her and quickly saddled, trying to keep up.

No one was there to check on me or tell me what to do. I kind of liked it. And it made me a little more careful. I must admit to being a bit intimidated by these people; very business-like, experienced, expert horsemen and women all around.

I was relieved when I went to mount her. She stood still as granite; she was easy for a maturing, late-blooming wrangler to handle. I cradled the reigns in my right hand alongside the saddle horn and stepped up into the stirrup, swung my leg over and down, placing my boot firmly into the opposing tapadero. God it felt good; one of those once in a lifetime moments.

She was feisty; liked to do a little hop on her front legs, snort and twist her head; almost as if testing to see what I would do. She was perfect. I was excited and grateful to be allowed to ride in this country, with these people, upon this horse.

I was assigned to work with two mounted women who carried margaritas and whips. That was their description of themselves. They gave me the impression of growing up on ranches and could have once been rodeo queens. They were friends and related to the owners of the ranch. These ladies had gathered horses on this range for many seasons.

Though friendly and respectful, they mostly tended to themselves, which I appreciated. Not knowing me, they seemed a little unsure of what to expect. In one sense I was on my own. In another sense these gals were counted on to keep an eye on me in case this new guy got into trouble out in the lonesome, as they called it.

I took along a very compact little survival kit. I pieced it together from my time volunteering for search and rescue. It was nothing fancy; three ways to make a fire, boil water, first aid, signaling, and a few extra high energy snacks. Shelter was a jacket, slicker and, of course, a horse. I didn't know if I was being a little silly or a little wise. Most of these riders were traveling pretty light. Though my group had whips and margaritas; they didn't share.

After riding a short distance, we jogged at a fast trot up and down a whole series of rolling hills where pinion and cedar would sometimes reach out and nip at our legs. The hills were steep and challenging for the horses. Some of the ravines had treacherous outcroppings that would form cliffs that would intermittently run several hundred yards.

We were to make a huge arcing sweep toward the southwest, covering perhaps a dozen miles. Along the way we encountered a fenced border that needed some repair. We were expected to make note of the location so it could be reported to whoever would tend to it later. In several places flash floods had taken out the posts and left yards of barbed wire strung across washes that were often steep and rocky with occasional cedar and an abundance of sage.

Barbed wire and horses are a bad combination. Riding at a good clip or even slowly into a nest of barbed wire can create a world of hurt for both horse and rider. It can be a cruel slicing tangle for a confused and frightened horse. We stopped and rolled some of it up, placing it near the top of a withered old cedar tree—out of the way so it could be seen and maybe retrieved when fences were mended.

We were flushing stragglers; missed horses that were side-stepping the gather and feeding on the fresh spring grasses down in the coulees. These little ravines, sometimes with spring water, were a good place for horses to hide or get lost. It was a yearly task for these ladies to clear this area, to get them out of the hiding places, over the ridges, and toward the more level sloping ground that would eventually lead to the south pens.

These renegades would often hear us coming. In a quick frenzy you might hear hooves rattling against shifting rocks as they would bound away from us, over the crest of the next hill.

A few times, I was used to plug known escape routes. Then the more robust rider with her cracking whip would dash; Adam style, up and around the favorite horse haunts. The usual plan was to push them toward her sidekick. Then she would hand them off to me. Blocked, they would stomp their feet, shake their heads. With a little encouragement I was able to get them to wander off in the intended direction.

As the sun approached the horizon, my pony was beginning to get tired. She was stout, sure footed, very responsive. But she started to hesitate; not wanting to move very fast. Twice, I caught up and met up with the ladies, and reported my concerns.

Twice they shrugged me off saying, "Give her a good kick, she's just lazy, she knows what to do." So I kept kicking and she got more and more lazy. I was even given a quick, condescending suggestion that I should try posting and use my legs more so I wouldn't get bounced around so much. Then I wouldn't feel so tired. But it was not me I was concerned about; it was the horse.

Eventually, my pony and I came to a ridge where we could see relatively flat open ground for about two miles. The gals continued flushing out the last few canyons toward the east. I was on the right flank and could see some thirty to forty head ambling across the sloping plains below. I was to watch for any others being flushed out, and to keep pressure on our day's labor so they would continue south, and not try to turn back to the north from where they had been recovered.

My pony was whinnying and shaking with head hanging low. But, I was told quite sternly to get down to the crossroads some three miles below or we might miss a rendezvous with two other groups of riders.

I was given our groups' handheld radio, but the low battery made it useless. I think the queen's ego was coming out. She didn't want any razzing from the boys about missing too many horses; of not being able to collect and keep track of them. That's what it felt like to me; but I think that sentiment may have been exaggerated a bit. Anyway, at this point, there were horse tracks all over the range. The sun was getting low. It was just a short while to day's end.

So, I pushed my protesting pony hard, several times. Dutifully she would throw back her head and off we would go; meeting new arrivals coming out of the breaks, pushing them down the trail and down toward the little gravel road where we were all to meet.

Then, she stopped her trot, began stumbling, walking slowly with head hanging almost to the ground. She started wandering aimlessly, not responding to leg pressure or rein. Wobbling and shaking, she collapsed to the ground. I crawled off her as she rolled over.

I lay there beside her for a moment; there in the sandy loam with the sparse covering of dry grass I could hear my heart pounding and the sound of her slow, heavy, labored breathing. I felt the sighing breeze, driving the sweat from my clammy skin.

Stunned, shaken, numb, I began to gather my wits; did a survey of my own aching body, but no injuries were found. I climbed to my feet and looked down at her trembling body with her breath intermittently pumping through her nostrils. All day she was climbing, trotting, loping; hour after hour, being pushed—on and on. I felt ashamed, embarrassed, and wondered if she was going to keep breathing; if she was going to stay down.

I dragged the reins out from under her heavy, sweat-soaked body, and pulled on her halter. She didn't respond. I pushed and kicked at her a few times hoping to get her back on her feet. I began to realize what I had done. This beautiful, innocent, pure-hearted creature could have bucked me off; just quit and refused to run. But she kept going, trusting, yielding, giving me every last ounce of what she had to offer. But now she was done.

I had no idea what was going to happen next. I began to feel an immense burden for what I had done; what I had allowed this magnificent creature to do.

A few minutes later, I began to hear an intermittent flutter that grew clearer and louder. It was the unmistakable pounding of horse hooves. I turned to see the alpha queen coming full speed. Apparently, she had come looking for me and saw me from the ridge. She looked shocked and a little chagrined.

Together we somehow got the mare back to her feet. We removed her saddle and poured some bottled water in our hands and rubbed it on her muzzle. She began to lick her lips. After a while, we heard the rumble of a pickup truck with a horse trailer. Lady sidekick had gone for help. Despite our folly we got my valiant steed safely back home.

I must admit I too was a little exhausted; physically and emotionally, though greatly relieved. Number 2711, Sweetheart, as I called her, was checked out thoroughly and seemed to be sound. She revived quickly, enjoying an extra round of oats. She was given an extra day off from work.

I realized, as she lay there, that it was almost like a metaphor for myself. How many times have I mercilessly driven myself to do things that it was not necessary to do. High expectations can be a blessing to push one to new heights of accomplishment and victory; but at what price. I thought of the pattern of forcing myself doggedly into situations where I had little respect for the toll it was taking on my body, my heart, my soul.

I learned that, maybe, it's not quitting; it may be just backing off a little bit for a moment, coming back later refreshed, with a different perspective or plan. How many times have I pushed myself relentlessly, banging my head against that proverbial wall to no avail?

It was not that I don't have the heart and the will to commit. Sometimes I simply need to take a detour, regroup, and come up with a better approach. My pony had reminded me of a great lesson; one that I thought I had already learned, but had not even begun to take into myself. She had brought it to the forefront again; not to listen or yield to foreign voices; allowing them to override and discount what I already know. I vowed that from then on I would always pay attention and listen to my pony. She often knows a different way, a better way that we might go. She revealed myself to me through her magnificent trusting, service, and pain.

After such an ordeal you would think she would be a bit skittish or standoffish around me. But the next morning she came right up to me; bright eyes, trusting, ready to go. But she needed her rest. Two days later she was back in saddle again.

My next horse was a little different. He was a bay with some Morgan characteristics. Deep, rich bronze-brown with bold, black main and tail, black halfway up his legs. This horse was fast, powerful and in his prime. Three days ago he was running with the herd. He was selected at the last minute. Bishop directed one of the better wranglers to check him out. So, after ten minutes of fast gallops, stops and turns, it was decided I could handle him. Frankly, I had my doubts. He had a mind of his own.

On the morning when the guests were arriving to begin their drive, we had a problem. About half the horses had wandered off; spread back up in a northwesterly direction. Again, this was the place of rolling hills and ridges, fanning out like fingers into the flatter land below. All riders were directed to grab their saddles, stop the scatter, and reform the gather.

It was the same dynamic. Yes, horses could be driven back down along and over these nonparallel ridges; but they might simply hit the flat ground, and circle back around again. Three of us were placed along the two- to three-mile plain, to be ready to nudge the reformed herd; heading south, back to the pens; to block any attempts at swinging back up north.

Almost immediately one rider left, being called up farther north to cover a developing breach. The remaining rider didn't particularly like his assignment. You could feel the rippling beat of horses running on the other side of the ridge and see the dust rising.

On the radios, it sounded like a World War II air battle, a dog fight. Wranglers were screaming into their phones telling others which way horses were going, where they were stopping. Wranglers and riders were calling for help and for back up; passing along frenzied messages of where the horses were massing, as they bounded through the grass, sage, and general gramma. The drama on the radio made it sound quite exciting. My remaining partner was bored, so he left. Our instructions were clear and precise; so I stayed in place, as instructed.

My horse was having a hard time handling the excitement and tension. He would not stand. He wanted to join the herd from which he had just been abducted. It took all my strength and skill to keep him trotting and loping in a disciplined circle. If I tried to hold him or have him walk, he would rear up and try to run. I thought to myself, "This guy is an Adam Special." It was all I could do to keep him under control. He so much wanted to run back toward the herd.

A short time later, I saw my deserter bouncing back and forth on the ridge about half a mile away. He looked like he was waving and yelling. I was unable to figure out what he was trying to tell me, if anything. He quickly disappeared back over the ridge. Since I had been able to hear the radio, I figured if I were to go somewhere else, Bishop our "range boss," would surely tell me. Then again, I thought to myself, he might have his hands full. I was probably the last thing on his mind.

Then I saw them. Close to two hundred rampaging horses broke over the ridge and were wheeling around from the south and heading back toward the north from where they had come. They were charging right toward me. Frankly, I was terrified. I was way past my riding capabilities, especially with the horse I was on.

There were four to five leading the wedge-shaped stampede. I remember one horse in particular that was in the forefront. Though not being sure of what to do, I released my pony and we rushed toward the outbreak. I could imagine horses scattered over three miles and thirty quests with no horses to drive. I became resolute. They would be turned and somehow I would do my job; make it happen.

I don't know if I was inspired, or just full of adrenaline. But I rode. Rode hard. I shuddered a bit when I realized the horse was not just loping, but close to a full gallop, pounding across uneven ground.

Then, I felt him. He emerged from that hidden place; and somehow, literally, grabbed the reins. I could feel his legs, hips, torso, arms, and hands. He was leaning, flexing; riding with his whole body. Oh, how he could ride! What a gift it was to know him, and receive his intervention. Well, why should I be surprised? He lived much of his life on horseback, and he was a cavalry scout.

I found myself half participating and half watching, as Jeb galloped us across the range; zig-zagging, jumping brush and gullies. Balancing from his stirrups, leaning over the saddle. There was such precision, confidence, clear unflinching focus. Jeb let up a little, allowing me to be me; back in control.

I was flat out charging toward them; taunting, screaming, waving. The leader watched my display intently, as if making up his mind. He slowed and stopped; shook his head, started kicking and spinning. Then, moving at a brisk trot; he turned, headed south, toward the pens.

There were some half-hearted challenges, but the rest of the renegades, just slowed and followed the white leader back toward the south, disappearing into the dust and the anonymity of the main herd.

There was not a single earthly wrangler to witness the spectacle. After showing me how to really ride, Jeb let go. My horse was settling down. We followed a few stragglers down the vista and into the pens. I relaxed and began breathing deeply; a bit awestruck, yet playfully amused at what just happened.

As I bounced along, Jeb's mood shifted to being more introspective and full of compassion. Then, as the New Age Christians like to say, I heard his voice, "in my spirit." It went something like this.

"You shouldn't blame yourself for what happened on that Island in Scotland. You can take a gal out of the dance hall; but sometimes it's hard to get the dance hall out of the gal. I had the same trouble with her in Tombstone; and I love her still. But hell, I was too old for her anyway."

I did not see that coming. True or not; it sure made sense.

His presence faded. He departed. I rode to the pens and finished the drive.

It's alright if you don't accept this merging with Jeb. I understand that it might not be an easy thing to believe. But Jeb and I know what happened. We were there, together. We made a difference and turned the herd and shared a little bit of hystory.

I was allowed to stay on at the ranch after the drive was completed and the guests had gone home. Sombrero gave me the opportunity to work with horses ridden in movie sets by actors like Harrison Ford and Johnny Depp. Later, I wrangled a short, bit-part in a new film as a curmudgeon old cowboy who didn't much appreciate hippies cluttering up Aspen, Colorado, in the seventies.

After relentless requests, I eventually worked out a deal. A wrangler really doesn't want to get rid of his best horses. But, I took Sombrero horse number 2711 home and gave her a new name, Sweetheart.

She's mostly retired and has become the alpha mare to half a dozen horses in a tiny forty-acre pasture. She is well cared for and seems content. I will always hope to have a couple of horses around; even if they end up just representing old memories.

I don't ride much anymore. I don't hear much from Jeb. I think he worked out what he came for and has pretty much moved on. My horses are old. The older I get, the more fragile and unreliable my body becomes. But I might do the drive, again; just one more time.

It was good to move cattle; to gather and drive horses; to know the raw freedom of wide open ranges and the majesty and power of some of the Creator's finest masterpieces.

I love my horses; like them, I too am aging. We may all end up just becoming yard ornaments; living somewhere in an open-range pasture; near mountains that shine.

Meanwhile;

"I thank God, I was a cowboy; at least for a while."

Chapter Eight

Back from the Vortex

I was finishing up a trip to Tombstone, Arizona where I was asked to do an impromptu cowboy poetry performance at historic Big Nose Kate's Saloon. It had been many years since venturing anywhere near the Superstition Mountains. So I decided to take a side trip to a place called Gold Camp.

A few miles off the freeway, on a winding two-lane highway, I began wrestling with my fifty-pound dog who had become weary of travel. He decided sitting on my lap would be more to his liking than lounging in the back seat. After a short vigorous tussle, I was able to convince him to return to his blanket-lined berth. However, I failed to notice that though I was driving straight, the road had taken a decidedly robust turn toward the left.

The proper thing to do in such a situation would be to slow down; allowing the vehicle to run a short distance, onto and perhaps beyond the shoulder, before bringing it gently back on the highway. Of course, I did the wrong thing. I panicked and over corrected; jerking the wheel in a desperate attempt to get immediately back on the road. The pickup promptly responded; skidding back on the highway with great enthusiasm. However, there was a backlash, and now we were starting to fish tail, as they call it, while I was wildly wheeling one way and then another attempting to regain stability.

As will sometimes happen in such instances, time slowed down to a crawl; everything got incredibly intense, and more than a bit terrifying. As the vehicle tipped up on two wheels, I noticed what appeared to be a rather wide and thick-something; appearing out from between the roof of the truck and the top of the windshield. It kind of reminded me of a huge glob of white tooth paste. Then I realized it must be an overhead air bag, deploying. I glanced in the rearview mirror witnessing my canine buddy, airborne, flailing his legs frantically, looking quite startled.

In that instant I gave up trying to make any attempt at getting the vehicle back under control. It was clear that this was going to be a serious accident and it was going to be ugly. It flashed into my mind that this may be the last moment of my life. I realized it would be all right with me. No one was dependent on me, except my little buddy, and maybe we would make the jump together.

Although I would prefer a few more years, I have lived a full, magnificent life. A clear knowing came to me. I was ready to meet my maker with all the ramifications of what that might mean. I found myself trusting the outcome, whatever it was to be.

Behind me and to the left, I became aware of two beings of light. They could not be clearly seen but they could be felt along with the cloaked radiance that enshrouded them. Then, behind them appeared a stronger, even more radiant being of light. I heard Him say to the two other beings. "No, send him back, it's not his time yet."

I was feeling a little shockey. I was fine but my body was trembling. The blood began to return from the core, my essential organs, and back into my extremities. Broken glass was everywhere. I pushed, pried, and kicked at the door. It finally gave way, just enough for me to crawl out of the smashed cab.

I found my traveling companion standing on all four feet firmly grounded, motionlessly staring at me. I will never forget his gaze. He was completely centered; balanced, focused, riveted, whatever words that might describe him in that moment. He was totally looking to me for any kind of hint or clue. He didn't understand.

He wanted to know if this was supposed to be a bad thing or a fun thing. I gathered him up and held him for a while until he relaxed. I knew responders would soon be coming, so I found some cordage and tethered him to a fence post so he would be safe; so he would not run or get in the way of other people or traffic.

My luggage and camping gear were strewn everywhere. Apparently, we had flipped, then rolled two or three times. I remember the police officer being very professional—responsive and accommodating—just the kind of guy you would hope would show up in such a situation.

A lot of gear was thrown around, both in and outside of the truck. My laptop was found over one hundred feet away. Most of the glass released and shattered. But, we didn't have a scratch. The medical services people were convinced I would have some bruising and strained muscles. They cautioned me about symptoms of internal bleeding.

Neither my Brittany spaniel, nor I, had any injuries of any kind. In fact, I felt like I had the best spinal adjustment I had ever had in my life. A lot of minor tension and backache had apparently released, from the centrifugal force; stretching my spine, as we flipped and rolled at over fifty miles an hour.

My puppy stayed with me another two years until he died in my arms from heart failure at the age of thirteen. I must admit that he was a bit skittish about getting in a vehicle for several days afterward, but he soon got over it.

Whether there had been divine intervention or just good luck, the event brought my mortality into focus and gave me some things to ponder. If it was not my time yet; why not? Was there something I needed to accomplish or to do, beyond enjoying my life and the people that I would still meet?

Like most of us, I was born at a very early age. Although it's true that I don't remember much about it, I am guessing that when I popped out no one had an inkling of who I might be. So, I figure, I was just assigned a convenient name that was made up, right there on the spot; and eventually it became my legal name. (That was a subtle attempt at humor.)

Seriously, I came with a great hunger to understand the nature of God, and to discover my place and assignment as a soul in the earth; allegedly having a spiritual experience. This quest has always been my heart's dearest desire, and deepest craving.

For me, this is the holiest of grails; it is the one and only true life purpose. It is the essential dance of life, the quest that keeps me alive, moves me forward; forging each step of the journey— you get the idea.

Of course, there are a lot of assumptions in such an endeavor which may or may not be rooted in reality. I accept that as a possibility, and a responsibility.

It is increasingly clear to me that once you decide what you think God is, or should be; God often becomes, through faith, a manifestation with the attributes of your own invention.

Our faith manifestations may not have anything to do with reality; I mean actual reality, that cosmic force which truly is God—by whatever words we may wish to describe or name it.

Some even teach that god only exists, if you think god exists. So, if you believe (have faith) that there is no god; then does that mean god does not exist? Do we collectively or individually get to decide? I think not.

My prejudice is that there really is something out there; or in here, as the case may be. It is my prerogative to find it; embrace it; play tag, or hide-and-seek with it; and to celebrate and live within its joyous presence.

We all come stained with our own philosophical assumptions and perspectives of how we think God should be. We mostly respond in accordance within the context of our own cultural inheritance, personal yearnings, and preferences.

I know people, have friends, who resolutely insist that there is no god. To them, it is a bogus fantasy of the stupid, the ignorant, and the easily fooled. I have noticed that there are those who doggedly want to believe, and those who refuse to believe; both can become radicalized in the quest of proving their point.

And, I observe that this belief or nonbelief stance follows most topics of concern in this life. We tend to see what we want to believe. It is a rare thing to be truly objective, open to new, undetermined, ways of thinking and perceiving.

I often conclude that whether or not we believe in god has more to do with how we think god should be; rather, than whether or not god is. If it doesn't meet our expectations; our standards of belief or faith; then we simply come to assume there is no such thing as a god or gods; supernatural sources of good or evil.

And, obviously He may be a She; or exist in an inseparable embrace of the both, or the neither; depending on your chosen folklore. And, of course, some get mired down with the debate between the many, or the one.

Yes, I have associated with non-believers who spend a lot of time and effort trying to prove that there is no god. To me that is a bit peculiar. I wonder if there is some kind unconscious or preconscious fear that god might really exist—when they are betting to the contrary.

There can be an almost desperate desire to comfort themselves; by constructing paradigms of assurance that the existence of any kind of god could not possibly be true; in the same way believers like to comfort themselves by collecting paradigms of assurance that god has to be true; perhaps because they fear nothing is there.

And of course there are endless proxy battles, of my god's better than your god; a curious supposition if there is only one. And, I acknowledge and understand that most of us spend little time attending to these esoteric issues and live our lives, day to day, in response to whatever the realm right in front of us has to offer. Perhaps these are the more fortunate ones.

Logically, I think the agnostic has the better stance. Maybe it is true; maybe is not. You can always wait and see whether or not a god pops up, and research the prospects; thereby coming to an informed or experienced conclusion. I personally, have never had a problem with Jesus wanting to save my soul. That's always been fine with me.

I believe there is truly nothing to argue about. We will most likely find out eventually; unless there is nothing there, and we just cease to be. So in that case, what's the difference? I say trust Him; give the guy a chance. He just might become the best friend you ever had.

I have always known that God exits, whether it's the Sunday school, Jesus version, or not. For me, there has never been any doubt. It seems so natural, so clear, so obvious.

For me, the crux of the issue has simply been; what is the nature of God? What is the part that I might play within this wondrous creation? What does God want from me, if anything?

What are my talents and abilities? Is there a preferred plan or destiny? What is it? Should I know what it is, or just live, discover, or create it? Why is God known by so many different names? And why are there so many seemingly contradictory yet curiously overlapping ideas, stories, and myths regarding our perception of the Divine. Are there really many gods or just one god? Are the many gods just aspects of the one god?

Does all that even matter? Life might be better lived by stepping out and just doing it; rather than drowning yourself in a quagmire of paralyzing thought; seeking to intellectually grasp all the possibilities and outcomes before even beginning the journey.

Sometimes, the grand experience, the grand presence, comes in ways that are acceptable and therefore embraceable by those who encounter it.

Other times, it can come as a manifestation or realization of something that is totally surprising, unexpected, and veritably inexplicable; perhaps leaving you feeling a bit unnerved, but filled with awe, and with profound knowing and joyful appreciation.

Those conclusions, interpretations and explanations of these grand encounters shape the many religions and philosophical perspectives—as they are codified, sanctified into our scriptures and mores—thus shaping our political and social institutions, and personal behaviors.

These ways of thinking can and do serve to organize social expectations and discourse. They also provide guidelines for the curious and hopeful that have yet to encounter the Divine Presence within their own direct experience for themselves.

It is a fool who does not find value in the footsteps and maps left behind by those who have at least touched, if not actually found, the grail through their journeys. Through these trailblazers, you can more easily find your own sign posts; take the turns that will help you find your way; and validate your journey.

Ultimately, you must walk you own path, and drink from the cup that your creator has prepared for you; allow the well to spring from within your own temple of experience and consciousness.

Even those who have been touched by the divine are often left with conflicting and errant interpretations about what has been encountered. They wrap their encounters in an ever-tightening shroud of stagnant belief and faith which can become an encrusted shell that blots out the light and no longer serves them on any deep or satisfying basis.

Then, once again, rising again, returning again; comes the opportunity to discover and embrace the Oneness.

Though all the above conjecture may be true; ultimately, none of that thinking is of any consequence. In my experience, Spirit is never known by reason and intellect. It can only be known when Spirit comes whispering and sometimes thundering into your life. It manifests through the witnessing of an indwelling, ongoing, living connection.

After the fact, intellect can attempt to interpret and describe; but is never quite able to sufficiently understand, or control it. The intellect is the moon; it is not the sun. The sun may shine upon it, but it can only reflect the light. It does not generate or control the light. God is only comprehended and known through the experience of a filled, responsive vessel.

The intellect may desperately struggle and cleverly clutch in its effort to seize the grand prize; but the creator is not known through analyzing; categorizing, measuring, and sorting.

The proper use of the mind is not that of a decider and over-seer, but as a tool to serve—to serve the heart and the will of the soul. It is not a heart of emotion, yet there may be emotion. It is a heart of conscious awareness, intuition, will, and intent that along with proper alignment is an instrument that can be honed, shaped, and directed by a heart that is in harmony with that Oneness that has no beginning and no ending; having no gall, no malice.

In short, the mind must become as an aperture through which the divine can be known.

Read those last paragraphs again; slowly, carefully, maybe out loud. It's important. It's a seed. Allow it to sprout. Allow it to grow. If it has already flowered within you, you are a witness of what I speak; regardless of the dharma or drama through which you may have come.

In case there is any doubt; now you know how I stand on the matter.

You should also know that there are times during this life when I go missing. Sometimes it happens while sleeping and sometimes when waking.

I find myself drifting, dissociating if you will; but it is a rather peculiar form of dissociation.

I notice it mostly when I come back, so to speak, to my usual state of consciousness. In dreams, I will recall returning to familiar places that are as real and alive as the one in which I am currently writing. My memories are not necessarily absent from this present time and place; but rather memory goes missing from other times and places where I sometimes dwell.

It is as if there is an imposed amnesia regarding these other realms. However, when I return to them, the veil is immediately lifted. And, once again I instantaneously recall and reconnect with the people, places, and activities where there is a completely separate existence.

Sometimes, while falling into sleep or waking from dreams, there are a few moments where I do remember; fading glimpses and recognitions. What is remembered most is a feeling of puzzlement that I don't recall these places when I return from the other side. But, when I go back to them, it is as if I had never left.

I also greet others who periodically phase in and out of those other realms. But as my conscious mind recovers, that great door quickly closes and is sealed. And once again, I am returned to my usual awareness and preoccupations.

What is retrained is the sensation of a memory, of a returning and reconnecting to a life where everything is intimately familiar and happening in real time; with the ability to make decisions and alter the course of hystory.

Although the glimpses and impressions may linger for a few moments; the scenes and activities quickly fade while the mind clamors to clutch and control, like a mental stutter, to recall a lost phone number, or to put a name to a familiar face.

It's there. It's real. But, I can't quite grasp it. However, it is sensed and felt as clearly as the clean fresh scent of approaching rain, or the warmth of an unseen campfire blazing behind you.

It fades like the setting of the sun, ushering in a grand cosmic spell; once more descending, enshrouding any detailed knowledge or recollection in the great darkness of forgetfulness. Then, upon a different time, another episode emerges; and the conscious mind is awakened, aware, and immediately engaged once more.

I am repeating myself; saying the same thing in different ways; to hopefully be as clear as possible. You most likely get the idea.

One of these bits of connection happens during a dreaming state, while in a trance or sleeping. This one is a place that looks and feels like an ethereal realm, rather than an actual manifested world. I enter into a great library of almost unlimited volumes of treasured, cherished knowledge on every subject imaginable.

Sometimes, I recall walking through the great marble halls with tall, massive, ornately carved, hardwood shelving—replete with all recorded knowledge. Other times, I find myself taking or being handed a book by someone whose face and form I cannot see.

This is a visionary state that comes to me with a honey-colored, golden light that casts rich warm shadows, providing the necessary contrast to enable images to be seen. Over the life span, these soft hues have come to be interpreted as an experience that has to do with some kind of message or elucidation; perhaps a foreshadowing that is being offered as an edification; sometimes providing information about something that has been pondered over time, with great curiosity and longing.

In these visions I find myself reading, sometimes out loud, the most profound and marvelous truths. Sometimes the words in the books are composed of unfamiliar alphabets or languages that I have no trouble speaking and understanding. I struggle to focus to be able to recall the information—the message, the subject that so fascinates me and has my heart so full of passion and gratitude.

Try as I might, my mind becomes clouded. The cherished wisdom, the poetic words and sacred pronouncements become mute in my mind. There is a sense that what I have been exposed to is eternally there; absorbed into some unconscious knowing; and may well consciously emerge from my memory, downloaded at a time and place when it will be needed and understood.

I have been there many times. Though I forget, I at least get to savor the awe, the majesty,the beauty of the splendid halls with their libraries of forever.

Perhaps that is the message; to simply know that it exists.

These forgetful visits are different from the sensing, feeling, and knowing of the lives, and places where I interact with a Colin or a Jeb. Colin and Jeb are more like a joining, cohabitating and remembering; more like an active personal recalling and communing.

I would like to dispel any idea that I am continually and indiscriminately wandering around in some sort of altered, semi-conscious, dissociative state. These supernatural occurrences rise and fall like the tides; come and go like the seasons. Sometimes there are weeks and months without anything particularly unusual or eventful. There are both prolonged droughts and bountiful harvests; time to celebrate the many blessings within this life, this realm. A time for everything.

However, I bear witness, that as the years wag on, I embrace an ever more consistent and abiding presence that fills me with a peace and a knowing that is honored and cherished above all else.

Regardless of how many times I may fail or get off track; it always seeks me out, and draws me back. Many of you know this presence; for you too embrace it, cherish it, and rejoice in its fullness.

It can remain absent or hidden for days or even weeks at a time; then can emerge for only a moment or linger for hours at a time. It seldom becomes manifest when called, and can emerge when it is not expected—and there is no thought of it.

When it is absent from my awareness, it is easy to revert to feeling, and being a bit lethargic, or reclusive. I can slip back; become the old curmudgeon without much joy or enduring purpose.

But as time wags on, this divine companionship is with me more frequently, more strongly, and for longer periods. And, it will sometimes speak within me, with guidance or commentary of both the mundane and profound; while allowing me to take my own unproductive turns to learn from the contrast of my own mistaken, misunderstood choices.

When it first touched me during that sojourn upon the promontory of a Sacred Mountain; it became my most prized accomplishment and joyful obsession.

Now I have become as an elder of an always present but seldom recognized clan; methodically and patiently tending to simple, little tasks, that spirit entreats me to attend to as it wafts and weaves through my life.

This spirit mostly brings me comfort and companionship; as I remain increasingly astounded at how with the fluttering of a leaf, or a turning of a snow flake. The world can be a beautiful, perfect paradise with an endless journey of abundance, appreciation, and ecstasy.

And, it sent me back. Back from the vortex; back into this life. So, there must be more to explore. More to be done.

Chapter Nine

The Mecca Called Moab

I was being called to Moab, Utah, through the back way, as we used to call it. It is a short drive across the Colorado border from the place where my house and most of my possessions were stored. We would exit Interstate 70 onto State Highway 128 which is a shorter but much slower route. The road is narrow and uneven, often full of imperfections and hastily attempted asphalt patches. Shoulders are intermittently crumbling; sometimes making it challenging for cars to comfortably pass each other.

In places, the shifting, settling earth beneath the road bed creates an unintended roller-coaster effect. The road meanders through high desert, steppe-like grasslands, which are not often green. Most of the time, the grass is hibernating due to the abundance of many, long droughts.

It passes through the, once upon a time, frontier town of Cisco, which started as a site to support the growth of railroad infrastructure. There was never much there. Most of the old buildings have collapsed or have been torn down. Travelogues like to think of it as a ghost town. Once there was a general store, a saloon, and a shanty town for housing railroad workers and others, who found themselves lost in the quiet expanse of endless prairie.

Those of my generation may remember a scene from the classic movie *Easy Rider*, with Dennis Hopper, Peter Fonda, Jack Nicholson; and of course, other, less well-known actors. In the movie, the characters had taken a break from their motorcycle journey; and set up camp in and around one of Cisco's "abandoned" structures.

It was a film that threaded through the growing pains of what came after the "greatest generation." Of course, other cinematographers have used the derelict shanty town as a back drop for a number of scenes, usually involving modern-day outlaws.

The area is now being re-deployed as a sort of semi-remote, industrial site for the railroad as well as for natural gas and oil production. Almost all of it is owned through the hand-me-down corporate infrastructure of those who founded it.

I love this old road. It takes me back to memories of travels with my mother and father during my childhood; bouncing across the Territories, Pueblos, Reservations, and Nations of the most recent indigenous peoples that inhabit the four corners region. It is even reminiscent of the road between Flagstaff and Phoenix, as it was some sixty years ago, long before the freeway, and the explosion of populations, towns, cities, and technology.

After a moderate meander, the road forks southward until it rendezvous with the Colorado River. It takes you through magnificent, red-rock canyons and flat open vistas with spires, mesas, and mountains, beckoning through the often haze-filled horizon. The chocolate-colored river lumbers through its parched canyons leaving an emerald green ribbon; clinging to its thirsty banks.

This is an enchanted landscape where dozens of movies and commercials have been filmed, cut, and spliced; bringing adventure, mystery, and awe to several generations. If you have seen any one of a dozen John Wayne classics, you have been here. And the productions keep rolling right into the present and evolve into more modern genres.

However, you will now find a couple of pseudo dude-ranch resorts where "the Duke" once stood. The area has become a recreational mecca for well over a million visitors each year. Moab, a sprawling hamlet of over 6,000 souls, is just a short distance away, at the west end of this narrow, winding highway.

The area provides all the amenities and support services the contemporary adventurer might require. Activities include everything thing from camping, hiking, climbing, rock hounding, foot racing, horseback riding, mountain biking, white-water rafting, four-wheel-drive expeditions, ballooning, touring by airplane, sky diving, base jumping, and just about any other fun and crazy thing you might decide to do. Sometimes there is even an opportunity to ride a camel; perhaps in honor of the ill-fated U. S. Army Camel Corps experiment that once enlisted these dromedaries as pack animals.

There is a collection of festivals to fit a variety of cultural interests; such as art, museums, lectures, and concerts. My favorite is an annual Scottish-Irish gathering. There is also a smattering of activities for political antagonists and environmental groupies.

Of course, you can shop, enjoy food, play golf, and soak up sun just about every day of the year. There are also large and unique National Monuments and Parks in the area.

But alongside and underneath the modern Moab drama is an ancient and sacred land. All the activities and amenities are just an excuse for the conscious mind to have an acceptable purpose to return; to enable a physical connection in which spirit can work its magic.

The iconic, red-rock landscapes are an ancient record; ageless scripture written in earth, air, fire, and water. The curious geological features attract visitors from all over the world to touch something that is primal and enduring. It is a place of reconnecting and remembering; revealing and healing. It is all right there, right before you, if you have the eyes to see, the intuitive heart to feel, and the desire to unravel some of the obliterated hystory and enigmatic mystery. Archaeology has not even begun to explore this hidden kingdom.

Over the years, I have launched dozens of pilgrimages, patiently investing time and effort; resulting in the opening of paths of communication within this magical and transforming crucible. It was here where I was stirred to write cowboy poetry, commit it to memory, and begin to perform on street and stage. Reconnecting and broadening my intense love of western heritage has been one of the most joyous experiences of this life.

It is where I have oft returned in gratitude and celebration for the revealing and the elucidation of the treasure of wisdom and heritage; infused into the very core of this holy land. For some this is primordial land; alpha and omega.

Years ago, before my Susan's passing, I experienced a series of dreams. They were the kind of dreams that leave you startled when you wake. They seem so real that you believe you have been abruptly catapulted from your home to some strange unknown dimension; a dimension that turns out to be this present world in which we have become so utterly immersed.

Susan spoke to me from her Source connection, and told me that I was remembering the actual place where my soul had begun its original sojourn; my first incarnation in a flesh body within this earth. Her Source claimed that someday I would be able to find and recognize the precise geographical location.

Years later, after she had passed, I was driving through the vast expanse of what is now called the Canyon Lands of southern Utah. As is my custom, I stopped to refresh myself by indulging in a short hike.

Along an unmarked trail, I lingered a moment, gazing across the great stillness, admiring the landscape. There it was. I saw, recognized, and remembered. For me, this was the place where my spirit collapsed into the incredible density of this dimension. The place of my first indwelling.

It was the vision within my dream; the bifurcated spire, the triangular mesa. I even discovered several colossal foundation stones forming a wide, flat shelf that once supported an ancient temple that perched above the winding river, several hundred feet below.

That discovery transpired many years ago. And now, this day, was to be yet another unexpected event; one that would further expand the ever-evolving drama.

Scots on the Rocks is one of Moab's newest events. It remains a quality, Highland gathering; complete with marching pipe bands in full Highland regalia; an array of competitions, demonstrations, and entertainments sufficient to stir the blood of any Scottish soul. I came with my enclosed box-trailer full of the stuff needed to complete a booth along Clan Row, thus honoring my family heritage and Clan Chief in Scotland.

It was a gloriously beautiful day; bright, crisp blue skies with towering red-rock spires. The desert sands were alive with their rich, vibrant hues. I was particularly enjoying gazing upon the massive cottonwood trees and tamarisk rising up from the river, along with the little tributaries, all framed by lush, emerald green grasses nurtured by late summer monsoons.

I was emerging out of the canyon, bouncing along the narrow road next to a stretch of lazy, slow-moving river. The air was fresh and pure, nourishing to both lungs and spirit. The skies had been cleansed by an early morning shower that left everything looking and feeling fresh and alive.

I stopped at a pull-out at the edge of the road. It was the place where a large, square boulder acts as a sort of sentry to the entrance of what is called Professor Canyon. Standing above the river, I looked toward Fisher Towers, savoring the majesty of their lofty spires. Then my gaze was drawn beyond, toward the silver and green alpine peaks of the legendary La Sal Mountains.

In the mydst of a totally clear sky, I witnessed the formation of a perfectly shaped, lensatic cloud above Mount Peale. It took just a few seconds. It was a curious cloud. As I watched it, I began to feel a presence that I could not quite identify. It left me with the kind of feeling you have when you cannot remember someone's name and your mind keeps struggling to recall.

Keeping an eye on the tenacious cloud, I proceeded a little farther along highway 128, stopping at Hittle Bottom campsite, where I continued watching the strange, motionless cloud hovering above the La Sals.

There was an unfocussed gnawing that was starting to feel a little annoying. I knew that some UFO buffs believe that extraterrestrial visitors will sometimes create and linger within these odd cloud formations. It is also believed that this phenomena has something to do with electromagnetic energy in the earth, which would limit these manifestations to certain times and places, such as mountains and mesas.

Supposedly, otherworldly craft can be suspended within a slightly different dimension; using the cloud phenomena as camouflage in order to avoid detection. I was also aware of some early American native lore suggesting that "sky people" can sometimes be summoned through mental telepathy, enabling communication with these visitors.

It seemed a bit outlandish to me, but though just about anything is possible, many things are not particularly probable. The most riveting feature of this event was the perfect symmetry of this cloud, in the otherwise cloudless sky. It didn't seem to be moving, drifting, or reforming; expanding or shrinking; the way most clouds do.

Feeling a little foolish, I shook off the whole idea and with a little sarcastic incredulity quipped something like,

"OK, if you are really there, why don't you form another one just like it, next to the first one."

I didn't doubt that UFO sightings may happen to some people, but I believed they were most often glitches in optics, tricks of perception, or imagination. Then again, I knew that the majority would consider that much of the supernatural I have encountered to be downright bizarre; if not outright incredulous. So who am I to judge how people experience the multitude of manifestations within this multiverse?

I proceeded on down the narrow highway, being aware of the timetable I wanted to keep; to get checked in at the motel, unloaded, kilted, and set up for the traditional festivities. My busy mind began to fill in the details of what I needed to get done in preparation for the festival.

Looking up again toward the Mountain, I plainly saw a second cloud; just like the first, forming above the promontory.

I didn't know what to think about that. But, it felt like there was some presence, feeling a little vindicated. It was like I was being toyed with; responded to; contacted.

OK, so clouds are forming over the mountains; like that is something unusual? So next, I reengaged with something like—

"OK, if there is anything to this, let's see you do it again. Let's have three perfect clouds, forming a triangle."

With the La Sals out of view, I continued the journey through and past Professor Canyon; soon arriving at the thriving resort mecca of Moab. While unloading at the Old Spanish Trail Arena fair grounds, I once again, happened to look up toward the promontory. To my amazement there were now three, equal-sized, lensatic clouds formed above the La Sal peaks, floating in a perfect equilateral triade.

Along with this display came an internal message. It was an admonition that I had heard many years before in Tucson, when Susan's great adventure had just begun.

Plainly was it heard, from out of the depths of that intimate place from whence spirit speaks;

"Lest ye doubt."

In a few minutes, the three clouds dissipated and vanished in a sky that remained cloudless for most of the day. I stood silently upon the field, enjoying the festival, but thereafter having an eye to the sky.

The next few days I began to have some recollections.

The first was during a short stint as a camp counselor on Mingus Mountain, not too far from Prescott, Arizona. I was sitting with a friend one evening watching a particularly stunning star-studded sky, when a luminous disk about half the size of a full moon appeared from the top of the sky. It acted as if it were on a dimmer switch or rheostat.

At first, it was rather faint, then it began to grow in brightness and intensity. It became about as bright as a full moon. It quickly drifted downward, toward the horizon from the north, going south. Then, instantaneously it shot to the right at a ninety-degree angle toward the east. After the abrupt, angular turn, the glowing object once again became progressively dim, until it could no longer be seen.

The entire episode lasted less than ten seconds. I recall my companion turning toward me with an astonished look on her face. She inquired, "Was that a UFO?" I remember responding, "I think so." We didn't speak of it further, mostly for fear of ridicule.

I also recalled a trip through the Nevada desert to visit a cousin in northern California that I had not seen since I was a teenager. On the way back, I remember being lulled into a trance-like stupor as I drove across the monotonous, bleak desert with its long, straight, narrow highway.

I became disoriented and heard a buzzing that came with a vibration felt all through my body. I remember opening my eyes with a start, thinking I was dozing off to sleep while driving. A few miles down the road, I discovered I was almost a hundred miles farther along than I should have been.

It turned out that my fuel tank was still almost full, as if I had not driven the one hundred miles. I know that doesn't make much sense, but that's what happened. Because it made no sense, I dismissed it from my mind and forgot about it.

During another incident I was driving between Monticello, Utah, and Dove Creek, Colorado, headed east. The gauges on my dashboard started turning on and off and swinging wildly. Being concerned about a potentially serious electrical problem, I remember stopping at a little place west of Dove Creek, Colorado, to check things out.

About an hour later, I found myself driving into Dove Creek; but coming from the other direction, going west back toward Utah. I turned around and proceeded to Cortez without further incident. Ever since that time, I've been a little reluctant to take that route.

Once, while being screened by an airport security X-ray machine, I was called aside and asked about the small metal object located in my lower back, just above the right hip. I said I really had no idea. I rechecked my empty pockets. They asked me to pass through the machine again. It was still there. It was suggested that it could be some kind of shrapnel. I told them it was possible, but I had no idea it was there. They waved me on through to boarding. On subsequent screenings, there has never been an issue. It has never showed up again.

The most unnerving memory is of an event that occurred one evening while I was outside in the little pasture at the residence in Grand Junction. I noticed a very fast moving star; or a very slow moving meteor or asteroid; depending on your perspective. Instantaneously, I was suspended, unable to move. At the same time, it felt like I was high above the adjoining mesa in some kind of vehicle or craft, standing in a cockpit or control room of some kind.

There was an unknown humanoid being standing to my right who turned and looked at me as if surprised, or even a little startled. Then, with a wave of his hand the whole thing was over. The entire event took just a moment. But time and memory being the way it can be; who knows?

As I went back to the house my wife called to me. She had no knowledge of what I had just encountered. But she had that subtle and definite look upon her face; the one which appeared when the Source was active

Source quipped, "The fleet must be in; have you been playing Captain Kirk again?"

The reference was to the science fiction television series, *Star Trek*, that I enjoyed in my youth. She got my attention, but nothing further was forthcoming. Apparently, the banter was to punctuate and validate my experience.

I also remember the channeled phrase "You have already remembered that which you need to know."

There are other "rememberings," some from my childhood. But it wasn't until I encountered that trinity of lensatic clouds above the Manti-La Sal Mountains that those scattered memories began to come to the surface and coalesce.

Perhaps we are not a solitary species, alone in the universe. Perhaps something new was about to emerge upon my horizon.

Chapter Ten

Sky Kiva

I was in Utah, cascading along highway 46 with windows open, savoring the fresh night air. Shiloh, my newest coyote brother, was riding shot gun; stoically facing the wind with his moist nose sniffing, his short ears twitching.

Most likely, I was guzzling down a diet Coke or crème soda while chewing a few chips of beef jerky; which, of course, would be shared with my enthusiastic little buddy.

I recall it being a moonlit night; the sky particularly magnificent. Showers of shining starlight seemed to reach right down from the sky. I was headed east from Old La Sal near the Colorado-Utah border. I had hoped to return to Grand Junction through Naturita, Norwood, and Montrose. Susan's Source had always encouraged us to take more circular routes rather than direct ones, especially when we were on pilgrimage. It had been some time since I had traversed this route.

I like to recite and memorize poetry on these long drives and I recall working on something new. I believe this was the trip where I was formulating, "Cozy Cowboy Cabin." It's perhaps too long and a bit redundant. But, it's my poem; my story, and I like it. Was thinking of turning it into a ballad.

At some point, the thought of seeking out Spirit Eagle had crossed my mind. Chances were better that he would find me rather than I would find him. I met him long before cell phones, in what became the Telluride festival and sports arena complex. He supposedly came from a long line of "spirit talkers." He wandered around the four corners region looking for anyone that would listen to him; holding small intimate gatherings where he would chant and smoke; offering messages from his totem spirit guide. He liked to tease me with unclear messages and claimed that I was due for some walking between the raindrops, as he called it.

Sometimes his sense of humor was a little challenging. Spirit Eagle would say, usually with a grin, that he was half Hopi, half Navajo, and half Zuni. Though he was on my mind, our paths had not crossed for at least a dozen years. He had told me that someday I would find my own Sky Kiva; but I never gave it much thought. He was always making vague and somewhat irrelevant pronouncements.

As the miles droned on, I noticed that the gauges on the dashboard were starting to flutter, then they became lifeless; stopping altogether. Then, they popped back to life again. Given my hystory and previous encounters, I began to feel a bit apprehensive; especially since this was a different vehicle than the one in which I previously had the same experience

A chill seized my body and I began to shake. I took a deep breath and started doing some pranayama—yogic breathing. Stopping by the roadside, I took myself and my four-footed buddy for a short amble through the shadows of the moonlit desert. The walk settled me down and I became more centered.

I didn't know if there was an electrical or mechanical problem; but I was getting weary and had had enough. So I drove the pickup a hundred yards or so off the road to a primitive little campsite, hidden along a ravine next to some outcroppings. It was sheltered and welcoming. We had located it during our walk under the stars. It was obvious that countless travelers had stopped here and rested through the decades.

I remember gathering up just enough wood and loose brush to start a campfire. A simple meal could be rustled up from the well-stocked cooler that I kept in the truck. It's not uncommon for me to concoct a cozy bed in the back of the pickup.

The walk and the food had somewhat revived me. My little Aussie buddy was happy to be out of the vehicle and on the ground. After checking things out, he settled down and came to lay down beside me, as we both sat enjoying the flickering flames of the campfire. I may have played my harmonica or bagpipe practice-chanter for a little while. I don't remember.

What I do recall is eventually drifting into meditation. I came under the spell of some benevolent, divine force. It was very comforting; feeling much like the energies that were encountered during the rollover in the pickup, north of Tombstone. It came with a quieting, calming, protective intent. I became aware that I was slipping into an altered state.

I couldn't tell if this was a dream state or a real place; perhaps some in-between realm. My perceptions were slightly muted and clouded; but the place felt very real, familiar, and intimate. I drifted in and out of consciousness as if sometimes dreaming and sometimes asleep.

I remember waking. It was morning; the sun was rising, but everything was out of place. I was no longer at the campsite. I had been taken somewhere else.

Behind and up toward my left was a mountain range of snow-covered granite peaks. Three cascading waterfalls were releasing their swirling, bouncing bounty onto and through an alpine basin. This upper discharge braided itself into a lower labyrinth of wetlands; framed by quaking, shimmering aspen groves, interspersed with additional clusters of old-growth evergreens.

The waters gathered into a pond of perhaps one acre, fed by a stream that gracefully formed along a low-lying ridge before plunging swiftly downward toward a lazy, muddy river that meandered through a canyon, feeding the red-rock country below.

I was walking on a game trail that became a foot path that followed the edge of the pond. The area looked like it was being maintained by beaver. There was a plethora of protective willows and wetland grasses. I came upon a primitive foot bridge, crafted from three, stout, parallel logs of ponderosa that were covered with a carpet of rich sod sporting green-growing grasses. There was the scent of fresh rain in the air.

I crossed luminous, crystal waters and began a short ascent toward the ridge rising up on the other side. An eagle circled high above the promontory. I was vaguely aware of bugling elk; the screaming of a cougar. There was a fluttering of feathers that reminded me of the challenge of an iconic white owl during a pilgrimage from long ago.

Some hundred yards on the far side of the stream the path wound gently upward, behind tall brush, and into the crevice of a stone wall. As I approached, the wall began to dissolve. A heavy, wooden door appeared. The top was shaped in an arch. You could see faint chisel and axe makings that were made across the grain where the rough planks were hewn from native timber. The formidable little doorway was held together by attractive, but crudely forged, iron spikes, bolts, hinges, and angular braces. At eye level, in the center of this entrance, was a tiny, shuttered window through which utterances and messages could be exchanged.

I felt a swirling, boiling gust of wind descend around me and the ominous little door shifted, then sprung open; but only slightly, moving but a couple of inches. Something beckoned me into the intimidating darkness beyond. I placed my trembling but resolute hand upon the iron handle, pressing forward, seeking to discover what was on the other side of this hidden, abandoned gateway.

Step by step, I willed myself into the cold blackness of the narrow corridor. As my eyes adjusted within the darkness, I began to see a faint glow of subdued light. I stepped out of the corridor onto a stone platform. It was not much larger than the bed of my pickup. I was standing in the vestibule of an egg-shaped cavern. It stretched forward about a hundred feet with a ceiling that rose some seventy feet from the lowest part of the mostly concave floor.

At the opposite end was an archway which opened through a cliff. It offered a bird's-eye view of both far away mountains and the valley below. It was a different perspective of the same view I had seen from the other side; before climbing the path, and discovering the door. I had entered near the top of the small end of this dim, egg-shaped chamber.

On each side of the platform proceeding downward, carved from rock walls, were matching stairs. They resembled a pair of embracing arms or outstretched wings. I inched along and down the left-hand side which deposited me at the lower end of the structure. In the center was a spring-fed pool that had a faint glow about it, as if it had its own light. Then, I realized there was an opening at the top of the cave allowing rays of light to pierce the darkness and shine upon the water, thus reflecting a warm silvery glow.

To the left and right of the glowing pool was the repeated pattern of outstretched arms or wings, forming a semi-circular bench-like tier. It was sculpted from a floor that angled upward toward the back of the cave, and downward toward the large arched opening that looked out through the cliff face. That, once again, offered the view of snow-covered mountains in the distance and the red-rock canyon below where the timeless, slow-moving, chocolate river, with emerald green borders, made its way to a distant unseen ocean.

I was drawn to sit, cross-legged, on a surprisingly comfortable, large flat rock at the center of the ledge above the shimmering little pool. Across the water and through the archway, I had a clear view of the other world below. It was then, I began to feel the subtle warmth of the dancing flames of a small fire casting playful shadows across the patina of the cavern's ancient walls.

I was sitting with eyes closed, listening to the gentle gurgling, and dripping of water; the intermittent crackling of burning wood; the occasional chirping and warbling of quarreling birds with feathers rattling. There was the rhythmic sighing of breezes mixed with the scent of the fire's smoldering incense, wafting through sacred space. I was beginning to drift within the drifting.

I was allowing myself to become devoured by the humbling, nurturing presence of the Divine Force, alive within that single moment. My mind began to flutter in confusion, trying to grasp, control, and understand where I had been taken, wondering if I would remember.

An inner voice bade me to breathe deeply and relax, intoning, "We will help you remember what you need to know; what we would have you write in the book."

In my mind's eye I began to look about this lost, but now rediscovered earth cathedral existing between the raindrops; between the worlds. To the right and left, were seated wise counsellors, friends and adversaries, who were adversaries no more. Twelve brothers and sisters woven into a tapestry of spirit and power, unbreakable and unquenchable, who were here before the creation of the stars.

Within this cathedral's luminous walls were many gateways; entrances and exits, from and to, many times and many places. They were guarded by mythical thought forms and beings of diverse purposes and manifestations. I could as much feel as see them; some endeavoring to remain unseen, hidden; with others clamoring for emergence into the light with missions both sacred and foul. Some were from times yet to come; and some from times that still live though they are no more.

Gazing toward the west I felt the familiar presence of an old friend. As my thoughts and feelings reached for him, he emerged from a gateway in the wall. I saw him as he was and how he had become; his failures and victories, his hopes his joys, things he still aspired to do. This was Jeb. I had discovered the well from which he had come. I saw and moved into his connecting cave—the one within his mountain retreat where he once sat and thought of me, wondering about my purpose and origin.

From the wall in the east came the Scottish sojourns. There, I watched from within the standing stones of Iona. Here too, the doors had been opened. This was where I found Colin and Malcom; where tragedies were righted and amended, giving birth to new songs to be sung. It is where I stood and looked upon the cloisters and monuments, commemorating glorious times and deeds well done.

Many an ancient gateway had been renewed and reopened, from whence the healing and the revealing would spring forth. I met and greeted many a traveler; friend and foe, some yet to come, some already known.

There were glimpses. Glimpses into the Sacred Halls; the deep depositories, hollowed out caverns, along the canyon walls where the records and the treasures remain, yet untouched, undiscovered.

This was a gateway of gateways; a star gate from this world and to those beyond. From here, with heart-felt desire and divine grace, one could move into any time, place, or realm.

With many friends, many adversaries, and through many times and many places my soul has come. And for one blessed moment the veils were pulled asunder; it was remembered, all is well, and all is One.

Though there have been many adventures behind us; there remain many adventures before us; for within every ending is a new seed for a world that is yet to be born.

Things began to get a little foggy again; not sure where I was or where I had been. I opened my eyes; this council of twelve was still around me. I was coming back from wherever I had been; to wherever I was to appear; wondering from which portal I had sprung and to which I would return.

Sitting with eyes open—with strength and power, both left and right—I gazed upon rainbow waters within this Kiva, within this enchanted realm. I gazed through the fire and across the waters, stretching through the archway, wondering which way I was to go.

Then, with eyes wide open, piercing from the roof top, down through the fire, and into the Kiva I saw Him coming; walking upon living waters, Creator of the universe, sustainer of my very soul.

Down on my knees, mesmerized, riveted, recognizing, rejoicing, welcoming; that all pervading, ever comforting presence.

I was answered, once again.

"From within the vast reaches of thine inner universe, I am that Halcyon Cry which echoes within each and every soul. I am that which fills the void. I am, the Great I am.
"As souls are ready, I would come. Ask that which you would know. I will commune with all of thee. I will come again as the need will manifest."

There was a refreshing, cooling, breeze flowing over my exposed skin, and through my beard and hair. I was relaxed, rested, content, spellbound. As I looked into my little dog's eyes, I could see that if he could talk he would have a marvelous story to tell.

I was back at the campsite. It was late in the afternoon. It turned out to be the next day. The moon was rising. I slid out of the bed of the pickup, being stalked by a curious pair of ravens, perhaps seeking a morsel of food. I remember gulping some water, sharing some with little Shiloh and pouring the rest on the back of my head and neck.

Walking across the desert I began to become grounded, getting back in synch with my body again. I noticed how my new boots were scratched up and stained with water; there was dry, red mud, splattered on my jeans, scratches on my hands and exposed arms. Puppy, my affectionate name for Shiloh, seemed unusually settled; calm, and responsive. He tilted his head, staring at me intently with soulful knowing in his eyes.

Hearing some passing traffic, I eventually recalled; we were just a short distance from the highway. But we were along the back side (east) of the La Sal Mountains near Moab, Utah, along highway 46; which I could see once we got to the top of this little hill.

Somehow, I had thought we had stopped miles down the road, far past the La Sals and well into Colorado. At this point, I could not truthfully state whether or not there had been a detour. But we were far from where I believed we had stopped.

As I sat, thinking, remembering, I wondered; perhaps this is what Spirit Eagle had meant when he told me I would find my Sky Kiva.

By the grace of spirit I have been guided to remember this journey so that it could be recounted and written. Much is remembered and much is forgotten; and more may be offered again.

Chapter Eleven

Dialogues with "I Am"

After securing a meal and lodging, I ventured into the national park north of Moab and sat beneath one its arches. As the delicate little notes from my bagpipe practice-chanter echoed around me, I pondered the events of the last twenty-four hours. My mind was flooded with wonderings and questions. Responses came quickly:

It was explained that there is an actual physical location, coinciding with the earth's ley lines and geological meridians, where pilgrimages and ceremonies have been conducted since ancient times. Apparently, my being brought to that location contributed to an alignment by which an initiation could be induced. If I were to return physically, consciously, to the location, it would look similar, but somewhat different on the earthly realm.

However, the location is where the experience transpired, just the same. It was explained that here there are burials, artifacts, and records sacred to cultures both present and past; cultures from times long forgotten, and even purposely hidden from man's memory.

These are not places where the uninitiated should haphazardly search with curiosity. Those who have need, who have soul connections to these sites, who are ready for mentorship and communion within these ancient Kivas will be brought to them, in accordance with their soul's chosen path. For the rest, there would be nothing of lasting value.

What I had witnessed was apparently offered from another, but overlapping, dimension. The images and sensations were how my conscious mind interpreted the encounter. Energies were manifested and displayed in ways that could be symbolically and metaphorically understood, within limited earthly understanding and awareness.

It was intonated that this was but one of many timeless temples created within the astral and ethereal realms where Angels and Great Masters dwell. Temples, cathedrals, sacred space with their feet in the earth, and their spires in spirit; connecting the earthly with the heavenly; creating a bridge, a passage, a gateway between the worlds of the seen and unseen; the yet to be discovered.

From previous readings, I took this to mean that there could be angels and benevolent spirts; but I also sensed that they could also be post-human, and even extraterrestrial.

From time to time, it was given that I would be able to meditate, contemplate, think upon the experience and be brought back to that place where the seed of the Christ spirit dwells. There, in that sacred space, there would be opportunity for dialogue for communing in ways of being that the primal earthly mind is unable to fully comprehend.

Nonetheless, there would be dialogue freely offered; answers that though not always easily accepted, or embraced, could yet provide ways of believing and knowing that would eventually bring fullness and peace to the conscious mind. That upon those stilled waters the greater awareness of the power and grace that is of the spirit can be better accepted and known; manifested, blazing forth as has been promised in so many ancient prophecies, scriptures, and teachings throughout the eons of mankind's earthly sojourns.

It was repeated; *"He will commune with all of thee; with all the many facets of your soul being, adding to the glory and celebration of the always existing and ever present Lord, God Creator."*

At times, it seems that this Source wafts through my consciousness, navigating through an overly jumbled, wordy mind. It is perplexing to realize that these forces using individual personality and thought patterns as a conduit, can and do become inordinately skewed or distorted. And the response is a resounding, "Yes!"

It was explained that many constructs, thoughts, and ideas had been, were being, placed in my mind for some time. Though the initiation was primarily a personal experience, it was suggested that it should be shared. The writing of this third book is a way of not keeping the intellectual aspects of this light hidden under the proverbial bushel basket.

Through continued guidance this would now be an opportunity to offer a personal message of insight and clarity for myself as well as other contemporary seekers; clamoring for a fuller, more complete view of the nature of how spirit has manifested; and is continuing to evolve and manifest in this present time.

Upon reflection, it was confirmed that the egg-shaped chamber could be metaphorically representative of the earthly realm. Coming through the door and down into a physical, earthly body. The passages and gateways could be representative of avenues of connection to other people, times, places; perhaps the Akashic records which could be brought forward into conscious memory.

The twelve—advisors, counselors—could also be seen as representative of the twelve pair of nerves in the cranium which bring us all our senses and provide our avenue into the physical world.

The seat within the center of the chamber where I sat could be a reflection of the seat of the soul that through the master, pituitary, and pineal glands, somehow orchestrates one's beliefs and perceptions and can provide the connection between the physical and nonphysical aspects of the manifested soul. And, the light upon the waters, that third eye, as a shimmering pool, a diamond full of light in the center; could be seen as the indwelling of the soul.

It was suggested that I should not discount the doors, passages, the star gates; which do exist and at times are accessed within this earthly plane. It was affirmed that there was great value in the contemplation of these symbolic and metaphorical mental gymnastics for they reach deep into other realms of consciousness that are rarely accessed or known.

It was suggested that it is good to keep the curious, conscious mind busy with the fodder of the inexplicable mystery, until, through the busyness, the mind becomes weary and rests; finding its proper place as the tool, not the craftsman; so that the intuitive soul-mind can emerge, regain its influence, and reveal the way home.

It is all much simpler than many of us try to make it.

But above all the shamanic explanations and machinations, I was most enamored by the radiance of the one I saw coming out of the light and walking upon the water of the shimmering pool. The one that was introduced as: The "I Am."

So, I sought council, gathered my thoughts and my questions, draped my simple woolen blanket around me, and sat in meditation upon the rock, to claim the promises written in the scriptures.

For has it not been written, that He would meet with thee within thine own temple?

"As I am sought in truth and sincerity, the Father compels me to come. I am the One; the One they call the Lamb. As you have asked; so shall I answer.

I was the first of my people; sent out across the waters into a new realm, to participate in the creation of a new world. I was as the Adam. Many were to follow; to come after me and we multiplied and became fruitful in our new land. Through the eternities, we became forgetful and lost in our wanderings. Not that this was evil in its essential nature, for this was the plan from our beginning; to explore, to create.

We began to search, to struggle for a path back and through to our home of origin, to come full circle, to complete the circuit, fulfill the mission to make fruitful, the expanding void. Long and tedious was the questing, for the return, for the way back and through, from the Source which was and is our home of origin.

As I was the first, the leader, the first born; it became my purpose, my responsibility to lead; to find the way home. Few were the tools and little was the understanding needed to complete this task. But never were we abandoned or forgotten. Our Source remained close to us, around us, within us though we recognized it not. So many manifested beings and helpers were sent, known as angels by some, but also known by many other names, through the many times, civilizations and cultures. These came to form the teachings, the guidance; the scriptures, blazing a new path back to that which was our origin and destiny, which is the same.

After countless trials and sojourns the path was forged. I became the truth, the way, the light. Not that I was the one that you should find, but that the way had finally been opened. There had been established the path to the light. Each will have his own trials and obstacles, as the way is made back, step by step; but through the grace of our Source; our mother-father God, the way was made open, clear and compete and nothing in the heavens or upon the earth shall be able to close it.

Listen, once again. Like the trail blazing explorer and pioneer; I, with the guidance and direction of our Father; forged, discovered and revealed the high mountain passage through which we might find the way to complete our journey. It is not that I am the one that you are to find; but rather the path, the connection, back to our father, our Source. This is what will make us complete. This is the path that all must follow to discover the harbor, and complete the voyage.

As scripture has accurately recorded; do not call me good, for I am not. It is the Father within that is good, and doeth the works. And, you may be called to do greater works, even greater than I have done. Our father reaches out to all of us, each and every one. I accept your adoration, your love, your honors, but in truth it is our Source; the One God, to whom we owe and freely offer our joy and gratitude.

For as I am as the elder brother; so you too are sons and daughters of God and of the Children of the Light. The seed that is Christ is growing within you, and will blossom within you in this generation. It is about to spring forth as flowers upon the hillside in the spring.

Do not stand clinging to me at the door; clogging the opening to the tunnel, which with the grace of God, that I have forged. Rather, rejoice with me, and follow me through and out into the light that we might be reunited, that all who seek might be redeemed.

Because I was the one who opened the door to bring us in, so I was the one who opened a door to bring us out. Great honor have I received from the Father, yet He is the father of all, our All Father. Nothing is done except through His will, His power, His grace.

This is why I was sent away from you; not that I should not be honored, but that I would not be worshiped as if a personality, in a cult; but that the wisdom, power and grace that is manifested in Holy Spirit might be daily encountered, embraced and understood.

Hear, O Israel, the Lord our God is One. Can there be a separation between the Father, the Son, and the Holy Ghost. In the final accounting can there be a separation? For all is One!

Yet, there are those who struggle against the light, who battle valiantly against the force that would redeem it; for they endeavor to capture, twist and wield the power for their own vain glory; rather than surrendering to the infinite and allowing compassion to serve all their needs with wisdom and grace.

Those who resist or deny their very soul; the Divine seed, the Divine spark within them, condemn themselves to be released into a holocaust of their own creation. Yet, even then, through that testing in the fires, through the anguish within their own souls, they may yet come to hope, seek, and believe. From this can come the learning, the growing, the expansion out of the dungeons of a self-imposed hellish prison back and into the blissful realm that is their true home.

It would also be given at this time that, yes, there have been battles and struggles throughout the heavens as there have been in the earth. Many visitations, struggles between those forces, those entities coming from other worlds, times and places; some to be of help and others of conquest. But, God is not mocked;

the promises are true and after the crucifixion a resurrection will always come.

He will come in the skies for His people and there shall be no more death; neither sorrow, nor crying, for the former things shall have passed away.

The cross was my path and my burden; but these who resist suffer every day more than I did upon my crucifixion. Know this well. Without your own personal crucifixion, your own personal yielding to spirit which is Holy, there can be no resurrection. In this, is found the freedom for the revealing and the healing; the manifestation of all that would be desired.

Yes, for many I am God's representative to this world. Yet, so are you; by that Holy Spirit that dwells within you and would seek its recognition and manifestation. We are all co-creators within the image of God. Do not worship me, making my form an icon or a graven image. But rather, see me as the example, the archetype, a beginning; a first step of things yet unseen, not understood. Come, worship with me, with great joy and appreciation that the Great I Am wrapped in Holy Spirit would be found and known; dwelling consciously within all who diligently seek.

The Scriptures; yea the Scriptures. Know that these come in many places and forms and are not just found in one canonized collection of selected works. The Great I Am is always revealing Himself, to each generation. For those who would see, the whole universe is scripture; a witness to the wisdom and greatness of the Creator God. Yet from time to time, a vessel is needed to contain the waters of pristine spirit so that the thirsty might drink, be healed and have their eyes opened. Though revered; it is not the cup, but the spirit that is holy. The vessels, though made holy by the witnessing of spirit, always fall short of the true glory and often fall into derision and decay.

Spirit can come in many forms and many places. It cannot be fully understood by that which is the conscious mind; but can be felt and recognized within each and every indwelling soul. Though it can be resisted; sometimes with great anguish, it flows where it will and cannot for long be constrained in any one vessel.

I come to offer good tidings and blessings. And I shall and do meet with you; often, within your own temple, that crucible of your own physical, conscious body.

I will come again as the need will manifest.

I wish you to have life and to have it more abundantly."

As I write, the words are once more funneled into my conscious awareness; and I wonder, "Was it grace or was I dreaming … ."

The Anointing

Once again, it is autumn in the San Juan Mountains of Southwestern Colorado. The countryside is replete with the accompanying splendor of orange and gold upon the hills and ridges. Up high, the crags and peaks have captured the purity of new fallen snow. The conclusion of another year and the onslaught of winter is heralded.

This morning I stood upon the rock, encircled by the green and copper grass of a little knoll; reveling in the power and majesty of the promontories towering above. Healing, life giving, waters bounce and swirl within the rocky streams and emerge into a wide valley, abundant with amber-colored willows.

As the billowing mysts of the morning fog began to lift, I recalled and celebrated the faith and encouragement that Susan had offered me. I stood, full of appreciation and gratitude of that spirit; the Source, that forever beckons to me; the embrace, the extraordinary opportunity to have life and to have it abundantly.

Upon this sixteenth year of my beloved's passing I honored her transition by striking up my pipes and releasing their ancient halcyon cry; sounding *Highland Cathedral, The Rowan Tree,* and *Amazing Grace* into the mysts of the silent dawn. As the sun rose, shadows retreated back and away from the hills and valleys; the billowing fog melted into the moist mountain air from which it had been summoned.

The sacred presence descended upon me.

Holy Spirit—by whatever name you wish to call it—is real. There is something; perhaps someone; there. It is alive and mighty. It is totally intimate. It is beyond all conjecture and mythologizing. It is beyond all wondering. It has always been there. It is here, now; though our conscious minds may struggle to devise an ideology in order to grasp, to comprehend, to intellectually navigate, to explain its presence.

This presence is not bound by any cult of personality or dogma. It is beyond all petty religiosity and institutionalization. It cannot be induced by credentials or certification. No one has the exclusive franchise. No one book can ever hold its power. No one teacher can have all its answers. Yet, its grace and blessings continuously form a progression of sacred vessels that become the foundation of every teacher, doctrine, and religion.

It needs no name, but has been called by many names. It manifests as it will, when it will. It's recognition and communion is the purpose of our existence. It is the essence of our existence. Its promises are true.

It can blossom in some of the most unexpected places. It can comfort, guide, gently remind us, over and over again; it can help us remember what we have forgotten. It is our origin and destiny. It can be acknowledged in others who have also recognized it, or have at least sensed it.

I have always been able to recognize it, or at least sense it. Some say that once the presence has clearly dawned it permeates you for all time. There are claims that you will receive vast powers, even if it touches you for just a moment. Others claim that those powers can exist whether or not you believe or encounter it. Still others say that even if encountered, there may be no "powers" at all.

I don't know how others, the holy ones; prophets, shaman, sorcerers, yogis, apostles, evangelists, and messiahs experience it. I only know how I experience it. Any demanding intellectual debate of the subject often deteriorates into the seductive interplay of the duality; insisting to know, "Is it this; or is it that?" When indulging in the seductive battle of rigorous questioning comes the dissecting and splitting. At those times, you can be drawn back into a mindless quagmire of excited irritation or lazy lethargy and dullness.

As I continue along this path, it becomes clearer and clearer that our lives are indeed a process, not an event; a journey, not a destination. However, there are often significant events and turning points along the way; sometimes with dozens of little events of foreshadowing; heralding a time when the clouds part and answers will come. And missed opportunities will often return in other ways.

As a maturing traveler, I have come to recognize that the world flows, grows, and expands in an evolutionary way. Nothing of value comes forth spontaneously without first having been planted, sprouted, and nourished; long before the magic of the springing forth of the magical fruit. And it fades, often to be found growing and flowering in another time, in another place, in another way.

I don't know how the Divine is supposed to manifest. I only know how I have seen it manifest. My suspicion is that I shall always remain pregnant with sacred knowledge and that I have always been wrapped within it; whether I know it or not, or understand it or not.

My experience is that it continues as a gentle, comforting, guidance and healing; allowing me to progress at my own pace as I am both willing and able to accept it.

If not pursued it will probably not come. Yet, when it does come, it is a gift that cannot be earned. It is a gift that is eternally given. It becomes a relationship that is a partnership in a never-ending state of exploration. My hope is that it will continue to grow within me. Whether or not it ever blossoms fully is of no consequence; for it is already here. I know not if there are other levels and other meanings. All that seems meaningless and distracting to the fullness of this one complete and blissful moment.

Although there may be continual movement within the motionless silence, the gentle softness; there is no hurry; there is no rush. It moves within each thought and within each moment until our journey is complete.

It returns again and again, to remind and reclaim. It coaxes away from bitterness and calamity. It soothes and caresses. It shares its life, personally and intimately. It is forever forgiving, and often sends teachers and helpers. It comes from a place where the human soul can truthfully say, "I am complete and need no more … ." It is the peace that He promised.

I am surrendered. I am His; and He is mine.

Epilogue

Affirmation

I LIVE in a paradise, within a blissful presence that creates, organizes and sustains the universe and everything within it.

I CHOOSE to embrace this Divine Presence in order to discover the opportunity to participate in the creation of a world of beauty, abundance and joy.

I RELEASE and renounce all false beliefs, judgments and notions toward myself and others, in order to be delivered and surrendered into this Divine Presence.

I ASK to be guided and supported in the manifestation of my dearest dreams and desires for the highest good of myself and others.

I RECEIVE and accept with appreciation and gratitude all blessings necessary for the fulfillment of my goals and the realization of my Sacred Destiny

I TRUST that all this, and more, is already being accomplished; whether I understand it or not, or whether I know it or not.

I THANK my Lord Jeshua; the Christ Spirit, Ascended Masters, Angels, Saints, Teachers, Guides, Ancestors and Friends of the Divine Presence.

Now my Tale is Told;
and my Song is Sung.

Adesh Wodan

Selections from

Riding Between the Raindrops

Cowboy Poetry

Written By
Dennis "Duke" Hunter

Trail of the Cowboys*

Ya' know it's hard to express in a poem
The emotions that come to a man
When your pony you straddle
Sittin' tall in the saddle
And you take up the reins in your hand.

Ya' connect with your old childhood heroes.
Ya' commune with earth and sky.
Time seems to stand still
And it's more than a thrill.
It can bring a tear to your eye.

'Cause you know then what's really important
And you're right where you're wantin' to be.
When ya' ride out alone
The whole world's your home
And your spirit climbs high and flies free.

So if you're heeding the call to adventure
And you're able to follow my lead
Then go saddle your horse
And take that one sure-fired course
That will take you to what you most need.

Go follow the trail of the cowboys
And those that rode out before
'Cause with a good horse beneath ya'
Your cares can't defeat ya'
And like an eagle your spirits will soar ... .

Back in the Saddle

Well, if I'm gonna be a cowboy poet
There's one thing I must do.
Seems I should be ridin' a horse
At least every month or two.

Now it's not that I've never ridden
It's just that it's been a while.
I once rode horses in the mountains
But I wasn't much more than a chil'.

And though the Army's famed 7th Cavalry
Made me an honored life-time member.
Well, we never rode no horses
'Cause we just flew a chopper.

So, I got ta' thinkin'
I'll call that guy, Don West
'Cause I can ride his horses
And he can show me all the rest.

Now, it's not that I've never ridden
It's just that it's been awhile.
When I told Don of my riding prowess
He just got this funny smile.

He said, "Well, here's a halter
Go catch that ol' roan mare."
But when I turned to look at all them horses
I just stopped 'n sorta' stood there.

He said, "That's the one in the middle."
As he tried to hide his grin.
I said, "Now which one did you say?"
And he had to tell me again.

But I finally got her cornered
But then she stepped on my foot.
Now ol' Don didn't seem to notice
So I just had to stay put.

Well, that mare kept a' glarin'
With wary disbelief.
Wonderin' what I was up to
As I stood there grittin' my teeth.

Then she drug me over to this hitchin' bar
But at least she was off my shoe.
And now I was a' limpin' and a wincin'
The way them real Cowboys do.

Well, we checked her legs and hooves.
Got 'em trimmed up just fine.
'Course was Don did most of that
I just watched from behin'.

But I learned all about groomin'
Checkin' them eyes and ears.
Combing out those beautiful manes and tails
And dodgin' what come out of their rears.

We even got 'em wormed
And vaccinated just fine.
Except for when Don hollered
Ya' see, my needle pricked him
Instead of the equine.

When it came time for saddlin'
I was all a glow
'Cause then I got to find out
What I really didn't know.

When it came time for mountin'
That was quite a trick.
The way I hung on that saddle
I think it made ol' Don feel sick.

But then he introduced me to Walker
I got 'em groomed and tacked.
Got my stirrups adjusted
For that I had the knack.

Then Walker started snortin'
And crow-hoppin' all around.
'n fact he was still a' goin'
Even after I hit the ground.

But I got my reins right
And off together went.
'Course it was Walker brought me back
'Cause I was all tired and spent.

Well now I help move cattle
In the spring and in the fall.
Spent time on that ol' Baker ranch
Over there in southern Utah.

I help gather and drive over six-hundred horses
That's up on the Big Hat.
I ride over sixty-miles in just two days
So what do ya' think of that.

Now some folks might yet believe
That I am just a dude.
But when I'm up on Walker
I simply feel renewed.

Some might say I ride like baggage
And am just some strange old man.
But to me I'm a Cowboy poet
And I'm Back in the Saddle Again.

The Scottish Cavalier

(Chorus)
He rode like a Scottish Chief across the northern plain
Arriving by the grace of God his destiny to proclaim.
In quest of freedom and liberty was here he made his stand
And he played his pipes so boldly across the American land.

When he met Miss Hanna Graves
She soon became his wife.
They pioneered the wild Midwest
And there they made a life.

With seven children in a house of sod
They claimed their American dream.
This was the proudest Scotsman
The plains had ever seen.

(Chorus)

With sweat and toil and hardship
They stayed upon their land.
And thus this proud young Scotsman
Became an American man.

Now he wasn't much of a farmer
But he tried it anyway.
Then he decided to breed some horses
And he learned to make it pay.

(Chorus)

But he left his home and family
At the age of forty-four.
You see, his oldest sons had already gone
To face that Eastern war.

So he took along some horses and
Joined the Cavalry.
Ended up escortin' wagon trains
Through country wild and free.

(Chorus)

But by the time he got home to his Hannah
His treasure tried and true
He was so weak and feeble
That his life was nearly through.

But their love lives on in heaven's song
Where they embrace their victory.
For together they found their promised land
And lived both proud and free.

And he rode like a Scottish Chief
Across the northern planes ... .
And by the way, did I happen to mention
That this was my great, great grandfather
And I am proud to bear his name.

Where Cowboy Heroes Go

Twas' barely fall in sixty-one
Or maybe it was sixty-two
When an early blizzard blew in
Just to fuss for a day or two.

Now I was a high country mountain lad
And I'd seen this all before.
But I started to feel a bit uneasy
When those vengeful winds began to roar.

It circled around and hit us again
As waves of snow continued to drift.
Not even old timers down at the Roma
Could remember fury quite like this.

We sat and we waited there in the valley
Hoping that soon the sun would shine.
But all we got was more snow a' blowin'
With relentless winds that would moan and whine.

Now there was always good grass
Up in the basins high above timberline.
But now our horses were stranded and freezing
How would we get them down in time.

Then Oscar stood up, kicked back his chair
Sayin' "Hells Bells I've had enough.
We've got to get them horses off that mountain
Even though it's gonna' be tough."

He didn't know just when he'd get back
But he knew what he had to do.
He said not to worry for he was prepared
He'd done this before a time or two.

So he saddled up his jeep and headed up the hill
But he didn't have much luck
Only got past the first two switchbacks
Where he figured he'd probably get stuck.

He grabbed his knap sack and put on his jacket
And stumbled onto that foggy trail.
With old Nordic skies balanced on his shoulders
He strode into the white travail.

Well, he didn't get back for a couple of days
But he was leading the horses all in line.
He used Big Red to help break the trail
Even though she'd gone snow blind.

Oscar said he'd stayed in the cabin
The one with the roof caved in.
Said it was good to find them horses
But he wouldn't want to take that trip again.

They were up to their bellies in freezing snow
In a world all gone white.
Couldn't find grass or even water
We were grateful they were now alright.

He said it was hard to get the mule up
He was just too old and tired.
But he coaxed him along with a handful of oats
Otherwise he might have expired.

Oscar had brought them all back home
Each one safe and sound.
As he rode tall into that pasture
A small crowd gathered around.

I looked into his wind-burned face
All reddened and wrinkled with age.
I also saw into his soul
And marveled at this rugged old sage.

There was no Cowboy hero
Greater than this old man.
He had a way of knowing
Just what it means to be a man.

To face travail with courage and faith
To steadfastly do what you might.
Without fanfare or expectation
To simply do what's right.

Without excuse, without regret
To live both bold and free.
This revelation is remembered yet
For it was his gift to me.

I knew this was his last hurrah
As I looked into his heart.
He knew that I understood
And this was to be my part.

To understand and to remember
To keep this spirit alive.
And so I've crafted this special poem
As tribute to his well-lived life.

And sometimes when the snow is blowing
And it's really hard to see
And I don't know when the sun will come out
Or if it's best to get off my knees.

I remember my old friend Oscar
And I begin to smile.
I hope to see him one more time
In just a little while.

Somewhere about Telluride Mountain
High above that blowing snow
In that place reserved in heaven
Where Cowboy Heroes Go ... .

Jeb

It was on Look Out Mountain
Where I first began to remember.
It was within that old museum
Right there outside of Denver.

His trail name was Jeb.
It was the darndest thing
When first we did meet
It seemed just like a dream.

He was wearing buckskin
All tired and cold.
Sittin' by a fire
Feeling used up and old.

His hands were folded gently
Around a dented cup.
Feeling quite contented
Though down on his luck.

Yes he was old and wrinkled
With his hair still mostly red.
Sittin' and 'a thinkin'
Of the wondrous life he led.

Beholdin' to none
Was what he liked to say.
As I stood there astonished
And listened to him pray.

He was remembering Asheville
When he was just a lad.
Thinkin' of little Lissy
And all the fun they had.

Rode with General Sheridan
During that uncivil war.
Became a Union Scout
'Til he couldn't take no more

And though his uniform was mostly blue
And his cause was surely just.
When the battles were all over
He mostly felt disgust.

With fallen carrion soldiers
Lying scattered all about.
And his beloved home in ashes
He left the grand ol' South.

Spent some time in New York City
And even wrote a book.
Tried to make some political connections
But they never really took.

So he set out across the prairie
And forged a brand new path.
Loved a young Shoshone maiden
But even that didn't last.

For a while he was befriended
By both Cheyenne and Sioux.
But then he rode for General Gibbon
But only for a year or two.

Next he became a land surveyor
Still taking army pay.
But General Crook needed a scout
And pulled him back into the fray.

He tried his hand at ranchin'
But that just didn't work.
Even spent some time in Tombstone
Just before old Wyatt Earp.

Wandering ever westward
He poured out his life.
Now he was sitting quietly
Recalling glory, recalling strife.

He gets that funny feeling
And shrugs his shoulders again.
You see he's sometimes conscious
Of me a' watching him.

Through the Creator's grand mystery
In a multiverse so vast.
We slipped into a shaman's way
And met there in the past.

By walking between the rain drops
We found our way again.
And soon began remembering
All the places that we've been.

He comes to me in quiet times.
He comes to me in dreams.
He shows me times and places
That I had never seen.

He lives deep inside me
From a place long ago.
He watches here beside me
From a place within my soul.

He dwells in that in-between time
Through which we all must pass.
He shows me what endures
And what will just not last.

We sometimes ride together
When veils of time disappear.
He thanks you for your kind attention
So I can bring his story here.

He wants us to remember
How we used to roam.
All those wild and open places
That we loved to call our home.

And though his past didn't last
And his future seems unclear.
Those who ride with me and Jeb
Will always be right here ... .

Tar Paper Shack

Gazing through a shattered window
At a ruddy red magic moon.
Remembering the life that he once gave me
While humming his favorite cowboy tune.

It's a tar paper shack among the cedars
Cradled by bluffs of red rock stone.
Near a seeping spring of inspiration
Where cattle would bawl and moan.

With great desire and desperation
Built by his calloused hands.
Here beneath Bill Williams Mountain
He forged his sovereign brand.

Rusty bent nails hang on twisted hinges
Clinging to a rotted kicked-in door.
Stars shine through an open ceiling
Where sage brush grows through a broken floor.

This is where he pledged his fortune
It was what he was born to do.
This is where his heart had led him
The place where his dreams came true.

When he first came to the mountains
He was lusting after yellow gold.
But what he wanted most was freedom
And he found his mother lode.

Searching with gold pan and sluice box,
Betting on black sand.
Capturing a little gold dust,
Claiming his promised land.

He rode a roan palomino.
It could really prance and dance.
He was the envy of local cowboys.
He won it in a game of chance.

He hand tooled his own saddle
And made some bridles too.
Said he'd rather fix things used
Than to always buy things new.

He liked to push his hat back
And I'd push back mine too.
And chew on a fresh custom whittled toothpick
Just like he would do.

He was fond of saying
"In this life ridin' in high county is as close ta' God as ya' can get."
If it hadn't been for them damn cigarettes
Well he just might be here yet.

Right along here was his bunk
And mine was over there.
Crafted from hand peeled ponderosa
With a homemade table and matching chair.

Cast iron would clank and rattle
As he'd fire up the morning stove.
While I'd step out and fetch more firewood
Stacked up straight in a covered alcove.

Riders stopping by for coffee
Sitting by friendly flickering fire,
Sharing cowboy songs and cowboy stories
That would tease amuse and inspire.

Shuffling hoofs of restless horses
Trapped in a brush fence pen.
With haunting howling coyotes
Stirring them up again.

Here beneath moonlit heavens
Under sparkling indigo skies
Filled with childhood memories
That come with tearful cheerful eyes.

Those cowboy days with Dad
Had almost withered away.
But locked in the heart of a child
They were all resurrected today.

Ah, that belching bully – that bulldozer
Will clear his cabin and corral at dawn.
But cowboy days are not forgotten
And my dad's legacy still lives on … .

Cozy Cowboy Cabin

(Chorus)
I'll search for her forever
The one with the auburn hair.
When I cross that restless river
She vowed to meet me there.

There's a cozy cowboy cabin
Beyond this teasing trickster trail.
An enchanted bit of heaven
Where freedom's not for sale.

Cradled in alpine valley
With rock of red and rose
With waves of wild green meadows
Where cactus never grows.
A river runs right by it
With a pond just down the way.
Where the aspen trees all shimmer
And the deer come out to play.

(Chorus)

It's made from stone and timber
With happy humble hands.
Aged with many memories
In majesty it stands.

Showers of shinning starlight
Reach right down to the door.
A home of joy and passion
Where soul has need no more.

There's tack stored down by the paddock
Where winter's winds come cold.
With whispers of fallen cowboys
Once young, never old.

(Chorus)

Spirit fills the canyons
On peaceful sacred breeze.
Trees caress the heavens
With prayer on rattling leaves.

Up high on magic mountain
Blessed with ice and snow
With ancient mystic caverns
Where only wise ones go.

We'll meet there in the autumn
And claim our promised land.
Recover the ancient teachings
And forge our sovereign brand.

(Chorus)

In the evening of the journey
In the dark and damp and cold
It's easy to miss a sign post.
It's time for the brave 'n bold.

I'm gliding along on Walker
My gaited palomino pal.
That cabin's 'round here somewhere
Perhaps past this old corral.

I can hear the call of cattle
As they bellow bawl and moan.
My pony will not falter
He'll bring us both back home.

(Chorus)

That cabin's 'round here somewhere
We'll meet there are the door.
She'll throw her arms around me
And we'll know love once more.

On the wind I can hear her laughter
Smell smoke from an old wood stove.
That cabin's 'round here somewhere
Perhaps past that old oak grove.

Yes there's a cozy cowboy cabin
Beyond this backwards bend.
The place where I've been goin'
To claim this story's end.

I have searched for her forever
The one with the auburn hair.
Well I've crossed that restless river
And I see her everywhere ... .

Gentle Little Kids' Horse

She's just a gentle little kids' horse
That's what the young wrangler said.
A cute little roan sorrel
With a star upon her head.

She stood so still and peaceful
With a twinkle in her eye.
Just the perfect patient pony
For a codger such as I.

She saw the headstall comin'
Took that bit right from my hand.
When I tried to mount her
Like granite she did stand.

He said she's therapeutic
By gosh I swear he did.
They use her on a dude ranch
Where she tends to little kids.

I rode her in a circle
'round the old corral.
Loped her in a figure eight
And she gaited fairly well.

Ranch boss roared
"Get movin' there's horses on the run.
Round 'em up an' sort 'em
There's shoein' to be done."

"Farriers are a' waitin'
It's time for you to go.
Ya' hired on ta' gather
Now git' on with the show."

Three-hundred restless horses
Strung out over a mile.
We slowly eased up 'round 'em
Took us quite a while.

Then my pony started snortin'
An' throwin' a heavy head.
Did a funny little dance
That filled me up with dread.

Bouncin' through the sage brush
She began to fight.
Crow hoppin', twistin'
Right, then left, then right.

I clawed 'n scratched and hollered
Pondering my perilous plight.
Thought I got 'er turned
But then that mare took flight.

My reins were surrendered
As I lost control.
While she just kept 'a leapin'
Towards this creepy craggy knoll.

Well, I lay there in a rock garden
On a cozy cactus bed.
With a barbed wire shredded arm
That leaked a lovely red.

She sauntered back to see me
Batting big brown innocent eyes.
She nuzzled me so sweetly
As I plotted her demise.

Now my knee wasn't all that twisted
I still could hobble 'round.
So I climbed back up on 'er
She weren't gonna' keep me down.

Rod'er back to the sortin' pen
Where the ranch boss appeared.
Gave me a long lingerin' look
While all the wranglers cheered.

"You caused quite a commotion.
Looks like you had a wreck.
Thanks for takin' that sorrel.
She ain't been checked out yet.

You been ridin' ol' Quagmire
And there's sumthin' else to know.
That gentle little kids' horse
Shipped out two weeks ago … ."

A Wanderin' Cowboy*

Ya' know I'm feelin' restless
More restless everyday.
And I know I must be goin'
Though I'd really rather stay.

But I feel the Spirit callin'
With a knowin' in my mind.
And I know I must be goin'
A headin' down the line.

Where this trail may lead me
Well I cannot tell.
Maybe someday heaven
For I've been saved from hell.

But regardless of the outcome
I must keep movin' on.
To sleep beneath the open sky
And wake up with the dawn.

'Cause I was born for roamin'
And guess I always will.
Grass keeps lookin' greener
On the far side of the hill.

Life is an adventure
And I live it day by day,
With His star to be my compass
And guide me along the way.

And if our paths should cross again
I hope you'll nod an' say,
"There goes a wanderin' cowboy
Who does it his own way ... ."

A Traditional Cowboy Blessing

May your belly never grumble.
May your heart never ache.
May your pony never stumble.
And your cinch never break.

*(Poems Inspired by Don West)

Other Titles by Dr. Dennis L. Hunter

Telluride: The Sacred Valley

Within the heart of the San Juan Mountains of Southwestern Colorado, the author unveils an intimate chronicle of the evolution of a spiritual journey. Spanning several decades, the story offers a richly descriptive window into the conflicts and triumphs of a modern truthseeker. Returning to his childhood mountain paradise, the author begins to experience a variety of shamanistic initiations in which he rather dramatically discovers and remembers an ancient spiritual heritage. This revelation pries open a new realm of possibilities and contains some profound implications regarding both our past and future. As a devotee of both traditional and esoteric forms of religious practice, Dr. Hunter is a well-qualified commentator and experienced participant in the quest for things of a spiritual nature. His training in psychology and his life as a typical householder provide a particularly unique prospective from the cauldron of modern American mysticism.

Available in both soft bound book and ebook format.

The Priestess of Mokhi Maya

The Priestess of Mokhi Maya is a love story. Written from a husband's perspective, it is an intimate chronicle of the challenges and insights of being married to a woman who becomes a full-trance psychic channel. Initially, the Source of the readings explains that it has manifested in order to provide inspiration and guidance for those who would be as "the children of the light." Later, it is revealed that agreements were made before the current incarnation in order to resolve some conflicts that were affecting the soul since ancient times. As her abilities evolve, there is the emergence of an entity that becomes known as the Priestess of Mokhi Maya. This vibrant personality is a previous lifetime of the channel. Over a 29-year period there are many unexpected discoveries and twists that culminate in a heartfelt conclusion as the tragedies and triumphs of previous lifetimes are revealed and miraculously healed.

Available in both soft bound book and ebook format.

Readings On The Resurrection

One late evening, under a starlit sky, in the Sonoran Desert of Arizona, a woman became filled with intense feelings of energy and peace. As she drifted toward a semi-conscious state she began to speak involuntarily. It was as if something from another dimension was using her voice. The Source of these experiences explained that it had manifested through this channel (and others) in order to speak to those who would be as the children of the light. It has come to comfort, to teach and to guide this generation through a difficult transitional era. The Source initiated discourses on various topics and indicated it would continue to follow this format. There are no claims or guarantees regarding the validity or reliability of this Source. It is the publisher's wish to simply allow the Source to speak for itself.

Available in both soft bound book and ebook format.

Readings On The Feminine Nature

One late evening, under a starlit sky, in the Sonoran Desert of Arizona, a woman became filled with intense feelings of energy and peace. As she drifted toward a semi-conscious state she began to speak involuntarily. It was as if something from another dimension was using her voice. The Source of these experiences explained that it had manifested through this channel (and others) in order to speak to those who would be as the children of the light. It has come to comfort, to teach and to guide this generation through a difficult transitional era. The Source initiated discourses on various topics and indicated it would

continue to follow this format. There are no claims or guarantees regarding the validity or reliability of this Source. It is the publisher's wish to simply allow the Source to speak for itself.

Available in both soft bound book and ebook format.

Teachings of the Land

One late evening, under a starlit sky, in the Sonoran Desert of Arizona, a woman became filled with intense feelings of energy and peace. As she drifted toward a semi-conscious state she began to speak involuntarily. It was as if something from another dimension was using her voice. The Source of these experiences explained that it had manifested through this channel (and others) in order to speak to those who would be as the children of the light. It has come to comfort, to teach and to guide this generation through a difficult transitional era. The Source initiated discourses on various topics and indicated it would

continue to follow this format. There are no claims or guarantees regarding the validity or reliability of this Source. It is the publisher's wish to simply allow the Source to speak for itself.

Available in both soft bound book and ebook format.

Essential Teachings

A series of topical monographs.

Riding Between the Raindrops

A special collection of Cowboy Poetry written by Author.

Back in the Saddle

A Compact Disc of Cowboy Poetry performed by Author.

Western Gallery

Attic Bunk House at Sombrero

Cattle Ranch Entrance

Duded up for Drive

Homestead

Horses at South Pens

Looking for Horses

Out Buildings below Cliff

North of South Pens

Paddock at Sombrero

Pushing Cattle to Summer Range

Saddling up for Drive

Sombrero Ramuda

Summer Grazing Range

Tack Room

Horse 2711, Sweetheart

Scottish
Gallery

A Gateway

Abbotsford, Scotland

Edinburgh, Scotland

Hiking Ben Nevis, Scotland

The Abbey in Iona

Iona Church Entrance

Interior of Iona Church

A cemetery in Iona

Piping competition in Estes Park, USA

Malcolm's Castle, Perthshire

Abbey in Melrose

Praying Scott

Sir Walter Scott Memorial

Author in Garden at Hunter Castle

Piping for a Fallen Soldier

Canyonlands Gallery

Ancient Symbol from many Cultures

A Solstice Marker

Canyon Lands, Utah

A Hidden Valley

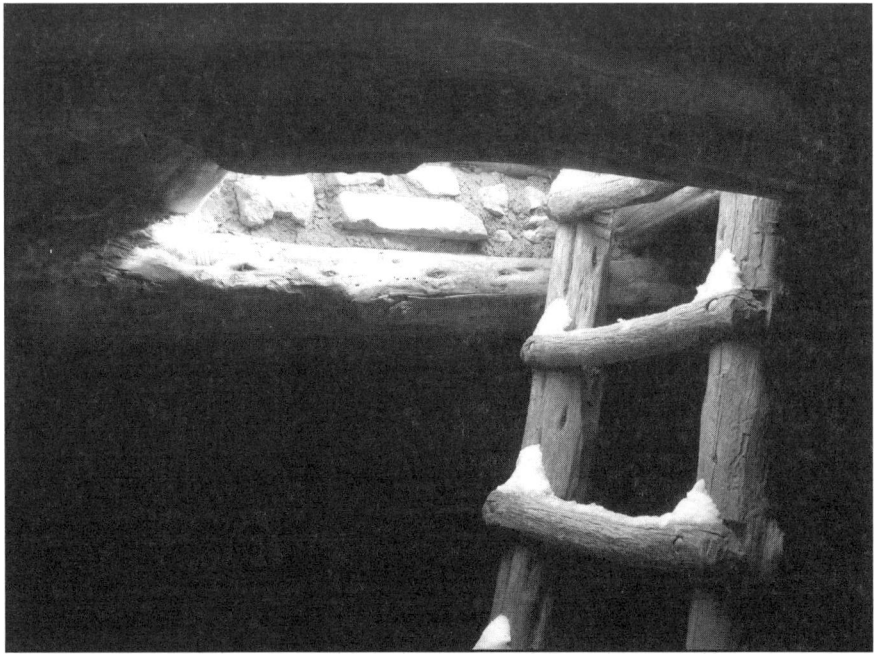

Passage

Dead Horse Point

Double Arch Moab

La Sal Mountains from Arches

La Sal Mountains in Distance

One cloud over La Sal Mountains

Two clouds over La Sal Mountains

Three clouds over La Sal Mountains

Lensetic Cloud over Grand Junction. "Lest ye doubt."

Twin Spires

"What we do in life echoes in eternity."

Marcus Aurelius